S0-BNT-185

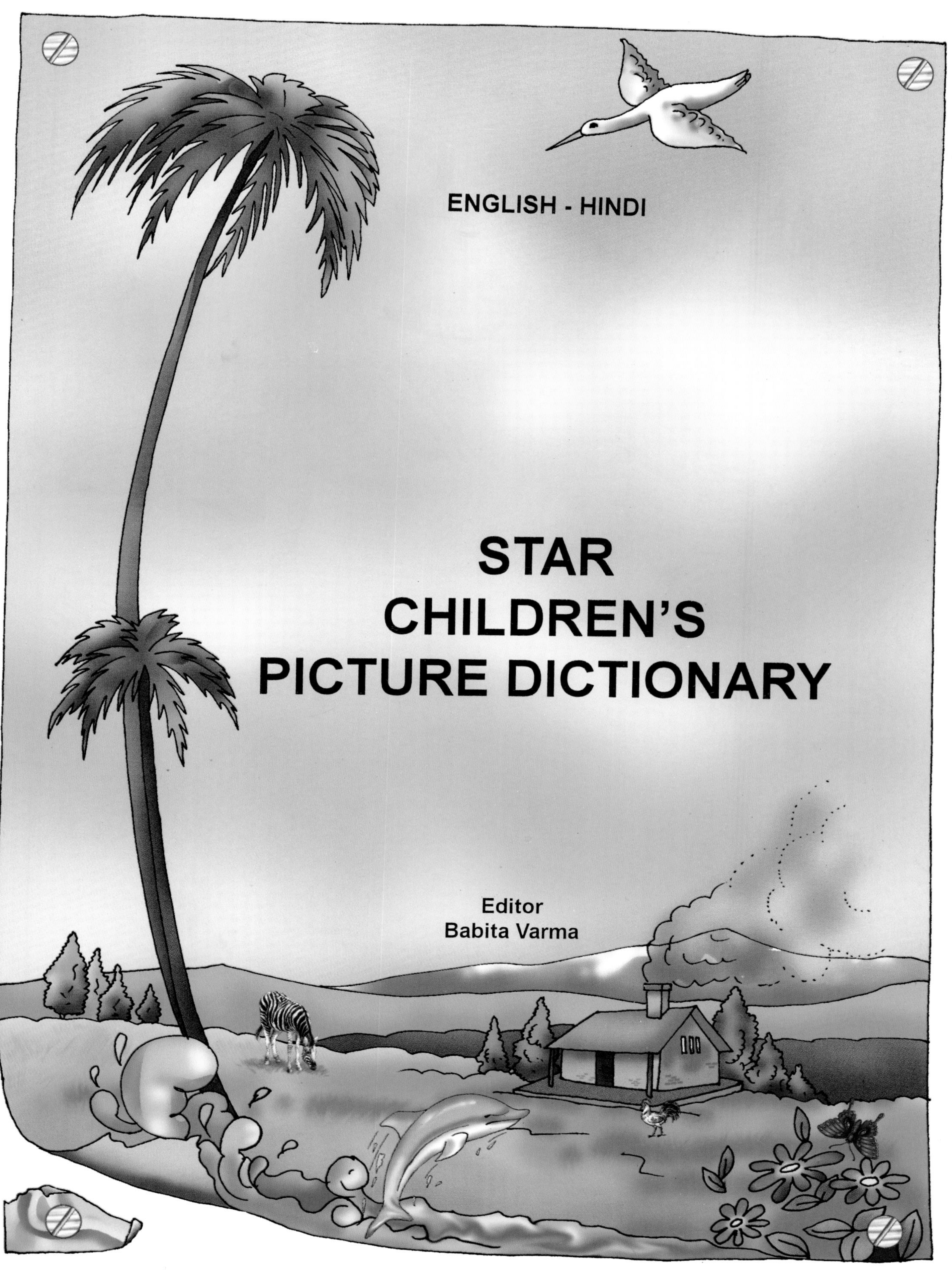
ENGLISH - HINDI
STAR
CHILDREN'S
PICTURE DICTIONARY
Editor
Babita Varma

STAR CHILDREN'S PICTURE DICTIONARY

Varma, Babita (Editor)

Published by :

STAR PUBLICATIONS PVT. LTD.
Asaf Ali Road, New Delhi-110002 (INDIA)
email : starpub@satyam.net.in

Revised Edition : 2006

ISBN : 81-7650-175-1

THIS DICTIONARY
has been published in Arabic, Bengali, Chinese, Croation, Danish, Farsi, Gujarati, Hindi, Vietnamese, Malayalam, Norwegian, Punjabi, Portuguese, Somali, Spanish, Tamil, Turkish and Urdu. Other languages are in press.

To
Children of all ages;
whatever language
they speak.

FROM THE PUBLISHERS :

This unique colourful dictionary was first published in 1993, and was brought out in sololingual, bilingual and trilingual editions. Within a span of three years we could publish it in about 32 major languages of the world, and the Dictionary was acclaimed as one of the best pictorial dictionaries to teach various languages-not only to young children but also to those foreigners who wish to learn another language. It was acknowledged as a source to build wordpower and stimulate learning, specially among children.

However, on the basis of various suggestions received since its publication, the Editor decided to revise the whole dictionary by adding many new words and illustrations, as also changing the style. We are now pleased to present this dictionary with a new format. This dictionary now consists of over 1,000 words and colourful illustrations, which have been catagorised in 12 popular subjects. In case of bilingual editions, each word has been translated into the other language, and transliterated where necessary.

We are confident that readers will find this dictionary as a very useful presentation which will encourage browsing, and make learning fun for the young and old alike. Since this dictionary has been published in several languages of the world, it will be found as a timely contribution to multilingualism and multiculturalism.

INDEX

HINDI ALPHABETS

अ	आ	इ	ई	उ	ऊ	ऋ	ए	ऐ
a	*ā*	*i*	*ī*	*u*	*ū*	*ri*	*ē*	*ai*

ओ	औ	अं	अः
o	*au*	*an*	*ah*

क *ka*	ख *kha*	ग *ga*	घ *gha*	ङ *nga*
च *cha*	छ *chha*	ज *ja*	झ *jha*	ञ *yan*
ट *ta*	ठ *tha*	ड *da*	ढ *dha*	ण *na*
त *ta*	थ *tha*	द *da*	ध *dha*	न *na*
प *pa*	फ *pha*	ब *ba*	भ *bha*	म *ma*

य *ya*	र *ra*	ल *la*	व *va*
श *sha*	ष *sha*	स *sa*	ह *ha*

क्ष	त्र	ज्ञ
ksha	*tra*	*jna*

	A a	B b	C c	D d	
	E e	F f	G g	H h	
	I i	J j	K k	L l	
	M m	N n	O o	P p	
	Q q	R r	S s	T t	
	U u	V v	W w	X x	
		Y y	Z z		

NUMBERS

0	**zero**-शून्य *shunya*
1	**one**-एक *eka*
2	**two**-दो *do*
3	**three**-तीन *teen*
4	**four**-चार *char*
5	**five**-पांच *panch*
6	**six**-छह *chah*
7	**seven**-सात *sat*
8	**eight**-आठ *ath*
9	**nine**-नौ *nau*
10	**ten**-दस *dus*

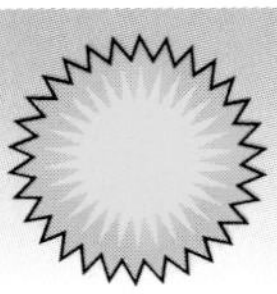

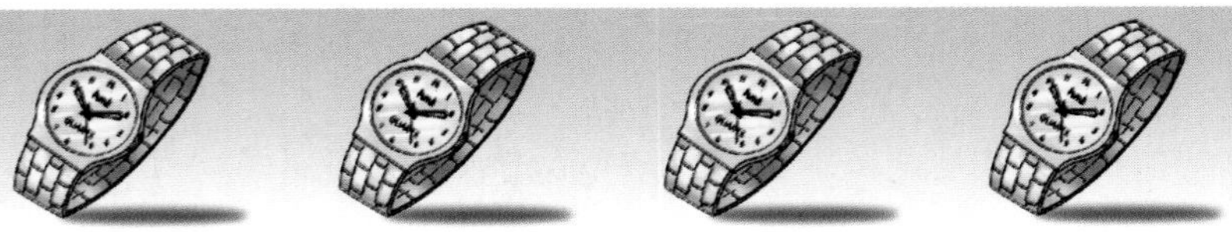

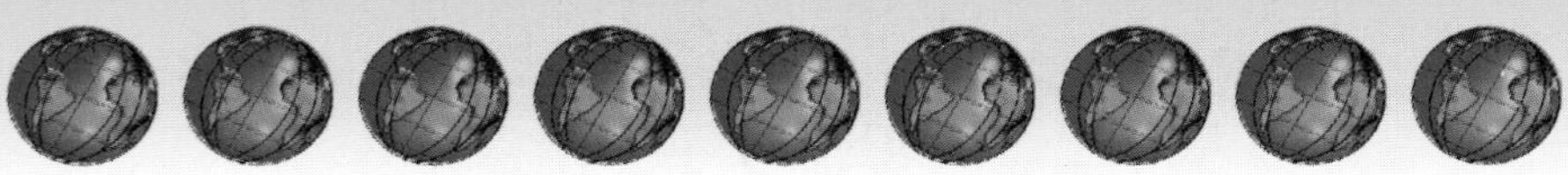

ANIMALS, BIRDS AND OTHER LIVING CREATURES

पशु, पक्षी एवं अन्य जीव-जन्तु

paśu, pakṣī ēvaṃ anya jīva jantu

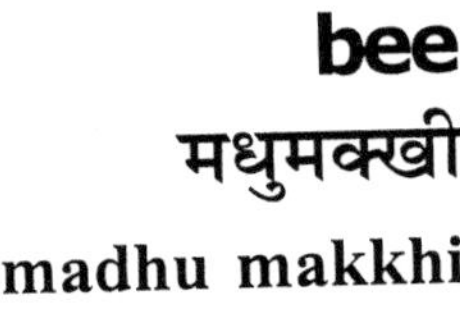

ant
चींटी
chinti

ape
वानर
vanar

bat
चमगादड़
chamgadar

bear
भालू
bhālū

beetle
गोबरैला
gobrela

bee
मधुमक्खी
madhu makkhi

bird
पक्षी
pakshi

bison
जंगली सांड
jaṅgalī sāand

buffalo
भैंस
bhains

bull
बैल
bail

bustard
सोहन चिड़िया
sohan chidia

butterfly
तितली
titali

calf
बछड़ा
bachhra

camel
ऊंट
ūnṭ

cat
बिल्ली
billi

caterpillar
सूंडी
sūndi

centipede
कन खजूरा
kankhajurā

cheetah
चीता
chītā

chicken
चूज़ा
chuza

chimpanzee
वन मानुष
vanmānush

cobra
नाग
nag

cock
मुर्गा
murga

cockroach
तिलचिट्टा
tilchitta

cow
गाय
gāi

crab
केंकड़ा
kenkarā

crocodile
मगरमच्छ
magarmachh

crow
कौआ
kauvā

cuckoo
कोयल
kōyal

deer
हिरण
hiraṇ

dinosaur
डायनासौर
ḍāyanāsaur

dog
कुत्ता
kuttā

dolphin
डॉल्फिन
ḍôlphin

donkey
गधा
gadhā

duck
बत्तख
battakh

eagle
गरुड़
garūḍ

eel
ईल
eel

earthworm
केंचुआ
kenchuā

elephant
हाथी
hāthī

fish
मछली
machhlī

flamingo
हंसावर
hansāvar

fly
मक्खी
makkhī

fox
लोमड़ी
lōmaḍī

frog
मेंढक
mēṇḍhak

giraffe
जिराफ
jirāf

goat
बकरी
bakarī

goose
हंस
hans

grasshopper
टिड्डा
tidda

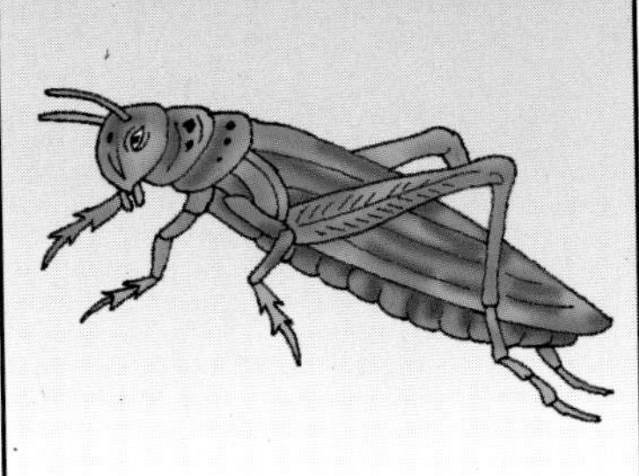

hare
खरगोश
kharagōsh

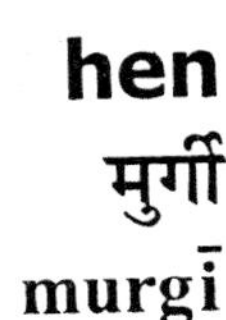

hen
मुर्गी
murgī

heron
बगुला
bagulā

hippo-potamus
दरियाई घोड़ा
dariyāī ghōd̂ā

honey- bee
मधुमक्खी
madhumakkhī

horse
घोड़ा
ghōd̂ā

insects
कीड़े
kīd̂ē

jackal
सियार
siyār

kangaroo
कंगारू
kaṅgārū

kiwi
किवी
kivī

ladybird
सोन पंखी
sōn paṅkhī

leopard
तेन्दुआ
tēnduā

lion
शेर
sher

lizard
छिपकली
chhipkalī

lobster
झींगा
jhīṅgā

louse
जूं
joon

magpie
मुटरी
mutari

monkey
बंदर
bandar

mosquito
मच्छर
macchhar

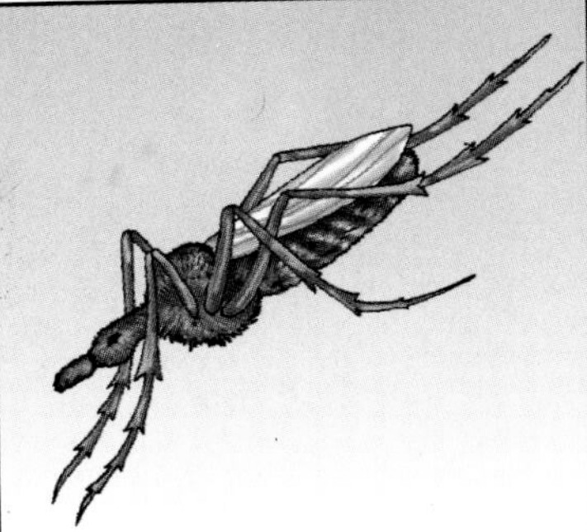

moth
पतंगा
pataṅgā

mouse
चूहा
chūhā

mule
खच्चर
khacchar

myna
मैना
maina

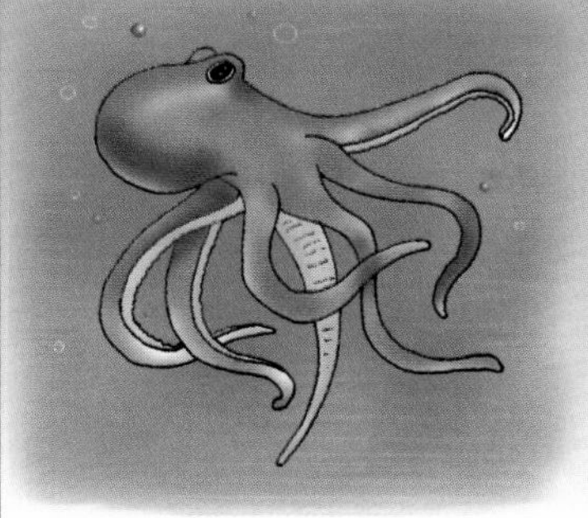

octopus
अष्ट पाद
ashṭa pād

ostrich
शुतुरमुर्ग
shuturmurg

otter
ऊद बिलाव
ūd bilāv

owl
उल्लू
ullū

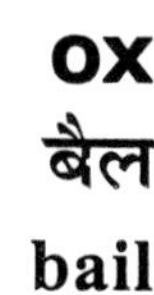

ox
बैल
bail

platypus
चोंच वाली बतख
chonch wali batakh

panda
पांडा
panda

panther
तेन्दुआ
tēnduā

parrot
तोता
tōtā

peacock
मोर
mōr

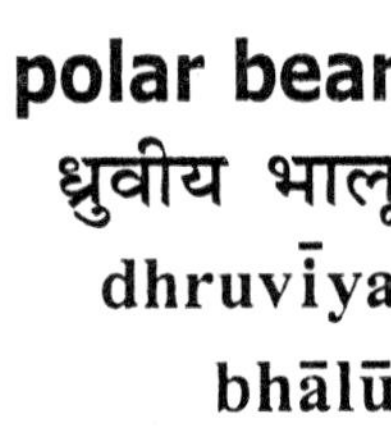

pelican
पेलिकन
pēlikan

penguin
पेंगुइन
pēṅguin

puppy
पिल्ला
pillā

pigeon
कबूतर
kabūtar

polar bear
ध्रुवीय भालू
dhruvīya
bhālū

porcupine
साही
sāhī

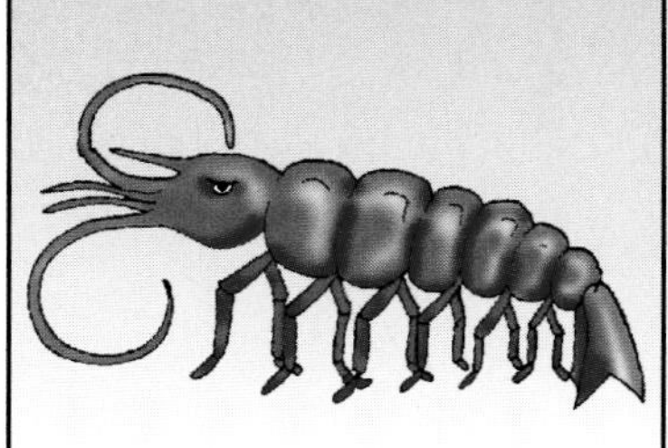

prawn
झींगा
jhingā

quail
बटेर
baṭēr

rabbit
खरगोश
khargōśh

rat
चूहा
chūhā

rhinoceros
गेंडा
gainda

scorpion
बिच्छू
bicchhū

seal
सील
sīl

shark
शार्क मछली
shārk
machhali

sheep

भेड़
bhēḓ

snake
साँप
sānp

sparrow
गौरैया
gōrēyā

spider
मकड़ी
makaḓī

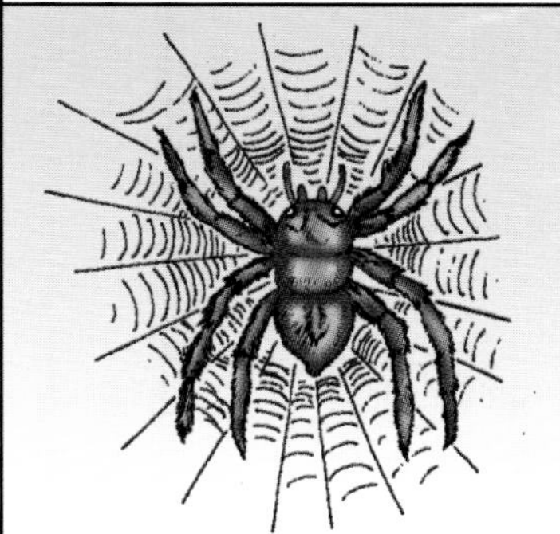

squirrel
गिलहरी
gilaharī

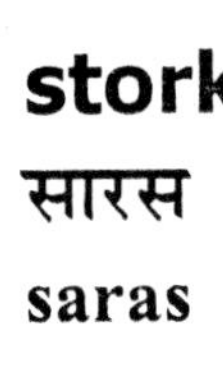

stork
सारस
saras

swan
हंस
hans

tiger
बाघ
bāgh

tortoise
कछुआ
kachhuā

turtle
कछुआ
kachhuā

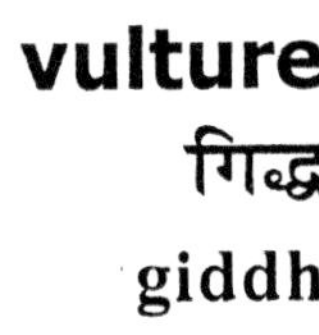

vulture
गिद्ध
giddh

woodpecker
कठफोड़वा
kaṭh
phōḍavā

wolf
भेड़िया
bhēḍiyā

yak
सुरागाय
surāgāye

zebra
ज़ैबरा
zebra

FOOD, DRINKS AND OTHER THINGS TO EAT

भोजन, पेय एवं अन्य खाद्य पदार्थ

bhojan, pēya ēvaṃ anya khādya padārtha

almond
बादाम
bādām

apple
सेब
sēb

apricot
खुबानी
khubānī

bananas
केले
kēlē

beetroot
चुकंदर
chukandar

biscuit

बिस्कुट
biskuṭ

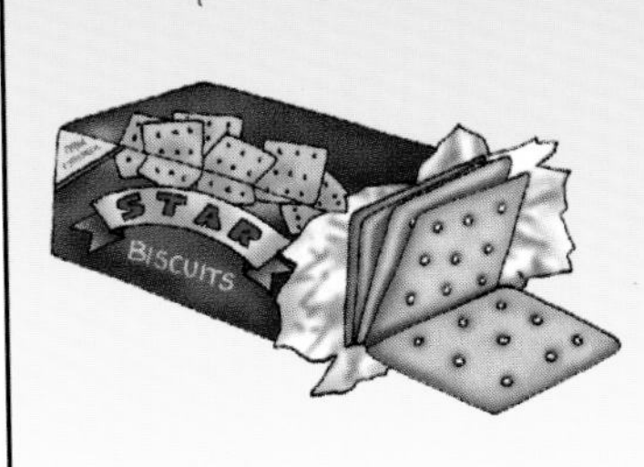

bread
डबल रोटी
ḍabal rōṭī

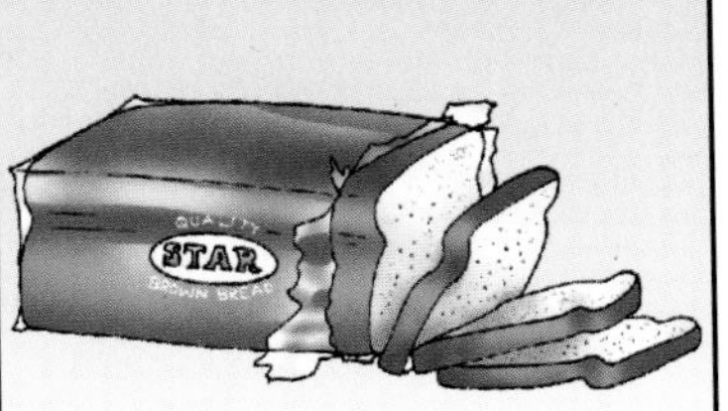

brinjal
बैंगन
baingan

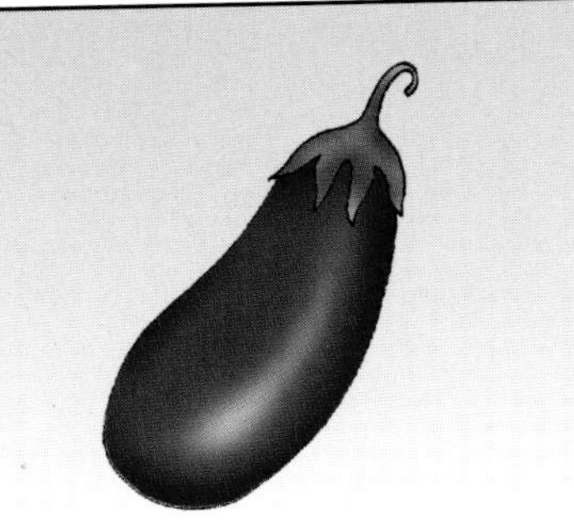

butter
मक्खन
makkhan

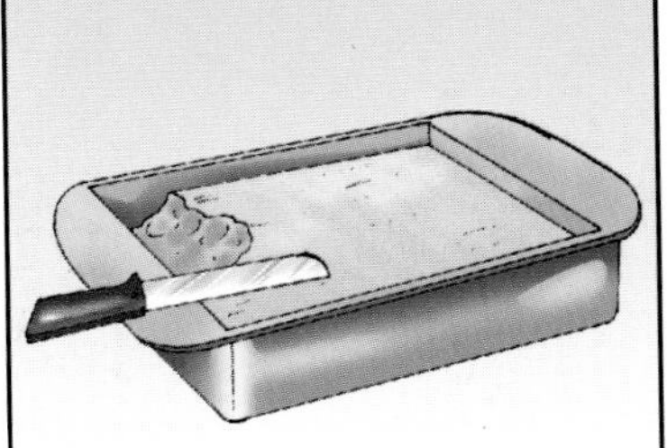

cabbage
बंदगोभी
bandagōbhī

cake
केक
kēk

carrot
गाजर
gājar

cauliflower
फूलगोभी
phūlgōbhī

cereal
अन्न
ann

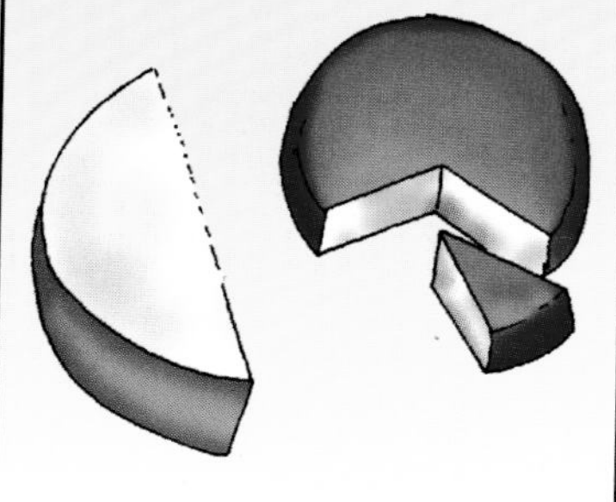

cheese
पनीर
panīr

cherry
चेरी
cheri

chilli
मिर्च
mirch

chocolate
चॉकलेट
chākalēṭ

coconut
नारियल
nāriyal

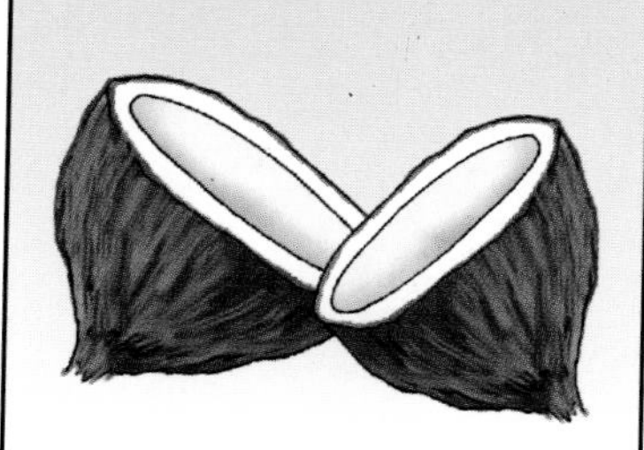

coffee
कॉफ़ी
kôfī

cucumber
खीरा
khīrā

currants
किशमिश
kishmish

dates
खजूर
khajūr

durian
फनस
phanas

egg
अंडा
anḍā

fig
अंजीर
anjīr

fruit
फल
phal

garlic
लहसुन
lahasun

ginger
अदरक
adarak

grapes
अंगूर
angūr

grapefruit
चकोतरा
chakōtarā

guava
अमरूद
amrood

honey
शहद
shahad

ice-cream
आइसक्रीम
āiskrīm

jackfruit
कटहल
kaṭahal

jam
मुरब्बा
murabbā

jelly
जैली
jailī

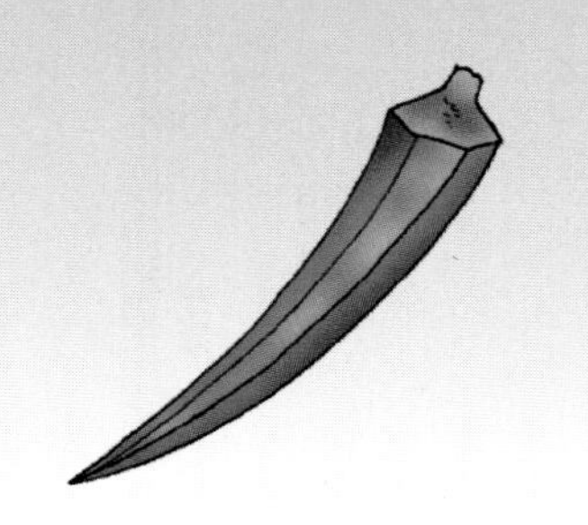

ladyfinger
भिन्डी
bhindi

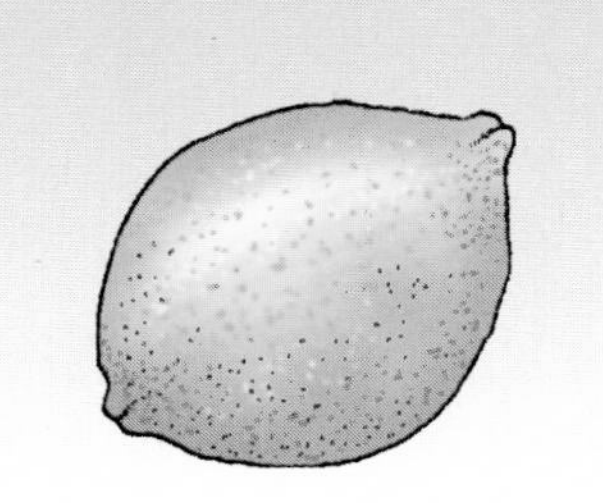

lemon
नींबू
nīmbū

lettuce
सलाद के पत्ते
salād ke patte

mango
आम
ām

meat
गोश्त
gosht

melon
खरबूजा
kharbūjā

milk
दूध
dūdh

mushroom
खुम्बी
khumbī

mustard
सरसों
sarsōn

mutton
मांस
māns

orange
संतरा
santara

papaya
पपीता
papītā

passion fruit
पैशन फ्रूट
passion fruit

peach
आड़ू
āḍū

peanuts
मूंगफली
mūṅgphalī

pear
नाशपाती
nāshpaatī

pepper
काली मिर्च
kali mirch

pie
नान कचौड़ी
nān kachauḍī

pineapple
अनानास
anānās

potatoes
आलू
ālū

pumpkin
सीताफल
sītāphal

plums
आलू बुखारा
ālū bukhārā

pudding
पुडिंग
puḍiṅg

radish
मूली
mūlī

raisins
किशमिश
kishmish

raspberry
रसभरी
rasbharī

rice
चावल
chāval

salad
सलाद
salād

salt
नमक
namak

sandwich
सैंडविच
saiṇḍvich

sausages
गुलमा
gulma

soup
शोरबा
shorba

soyabeans
सोयाबीन
sōyābīn

spaghetti
स्पाघेटी
spāghēṭī

spinach
पालक
pālak

strawberry
हिसालू
hisālū

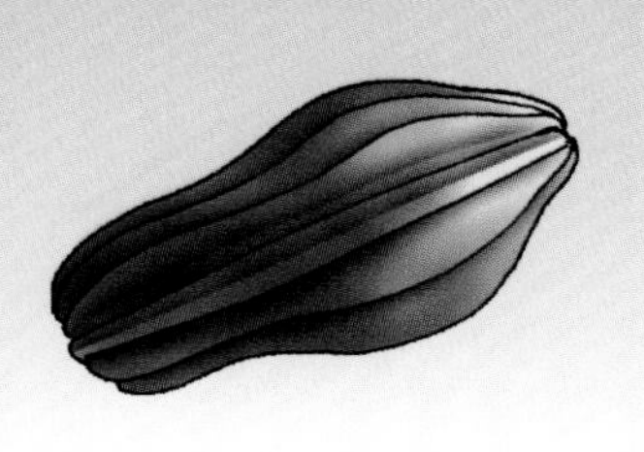

starfruit
स्टारफल
starphal

sugar
चीनी
chīnī

sweet potatoes
शकरकंद
shakarkand

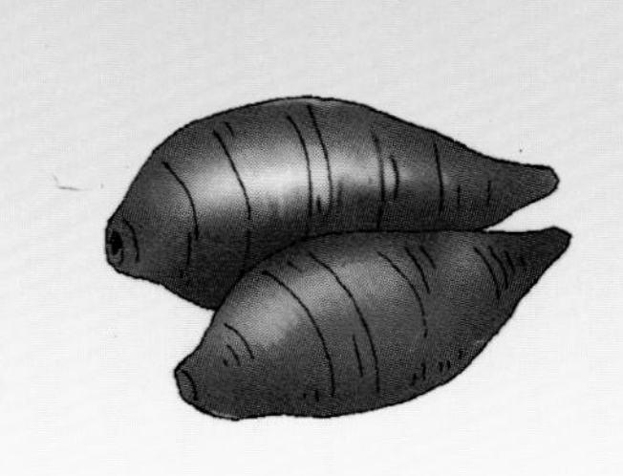

sweet
मिठाई
mithai

sweetcorn
मक्की
makkī

syrup
शरबत
sharbat

tea
चाय
chāi

toast
टोस्ट
ṭōsṭ

toffee
टॉफ़ी
ṭôfī

tomato
टमाटर
tamater

turnip
शलजम
shaljam

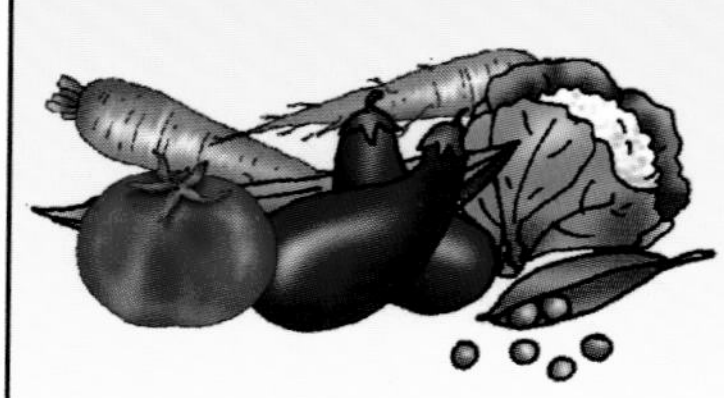

vegetables
सब्ज़ी
sabzi

walnut
अखरोट
akhrōṭ

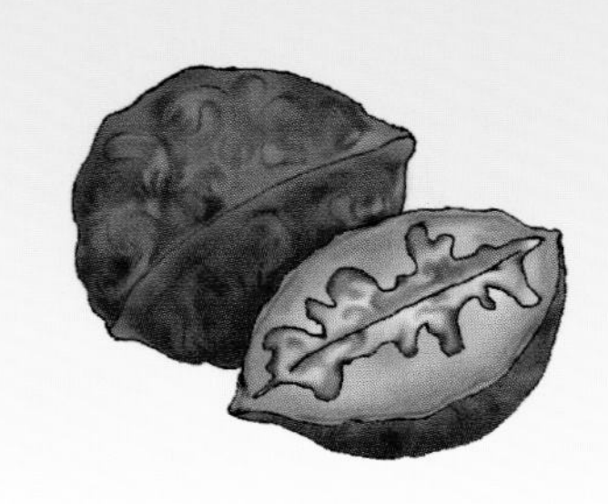

water
पानी
pānī

watermelon
तरबूज़
tarbuz

wheat
गेहूँ
gēnhū

yoghurt
दही
dahī

HOME

घर

ghar

antenna
एरियल
ēriyal

balcony
छज्जा
chhajja

basin
चिलमची
chilamchi

bathroom
स्नानागार
snānāgār

bed
बिस्तर
bistar

bedroom
शयनागार
shayanāgār

bench
बैंच, तख्त
baiñch, takht

blanket
कंबल
kambal

bucket
बाल्टी
bālṭī

cabinet
अलमारी
almārī

carpet
कालीन
kālīn

ceiling
छत
chhat

chair
कुर्सी
kursī

chandelier
फानूस
fanus

chimney
चिमनी
chimney

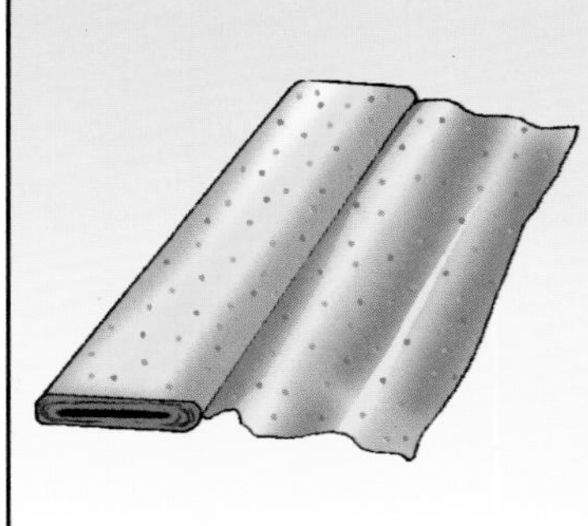

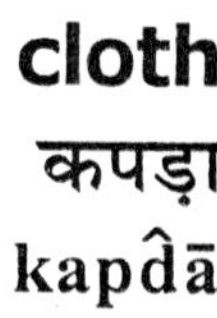

cloth
कपड़ा
kapḍā

cot
पलंग
palang

cupboard
अलमारी
almārī

curtain
पर्दा
parda

door
दरवाज़ा
darvāzā

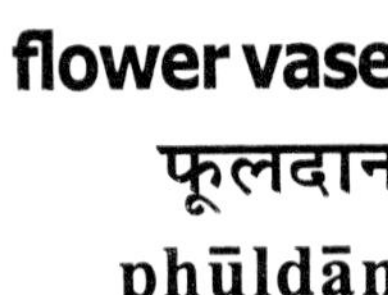

drain
मोरी
mori

elevator
लिफ्ट
lift

escalator
विद्युत सीढ़ी
vidyut sīd̂hī

fences
बाड़ा
bād̂ā

flats
फ्लैट्स
flats

flower vase
फूलदान
phūldān

foam
फोम रबड़
fōm rabad̂

fork
कांटा
kāṇṭā

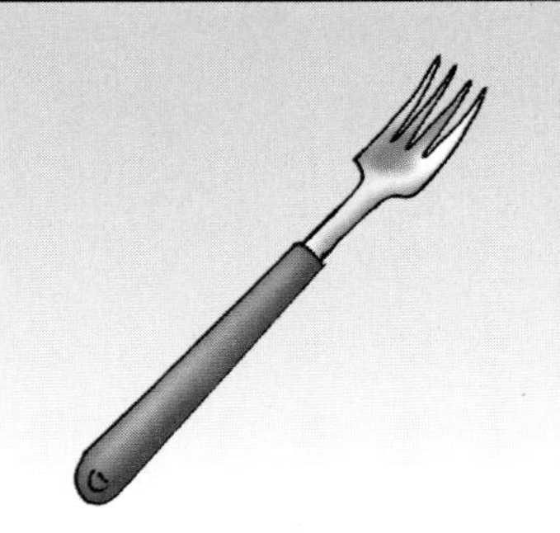

garden
उद्यान
udyān

garage
मोटर खाना
mōṭar
khānā

gate
दरवाज़ा
darvāzā

home
घर
ghar

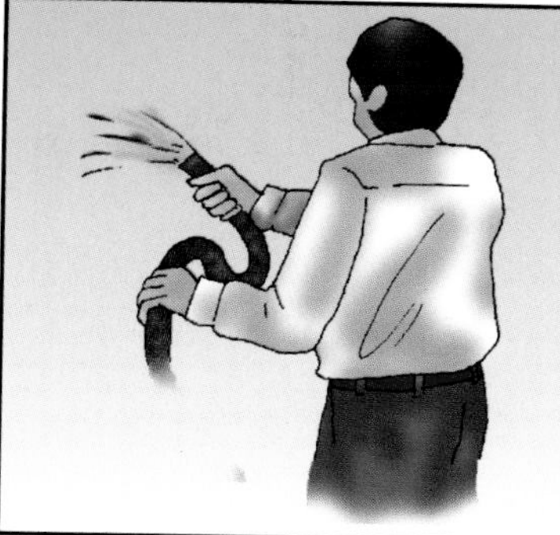

hose
नली
nali

kitchen
रसोई
rasoī

letter-box
पत्र-पेटी
patr pēṭī

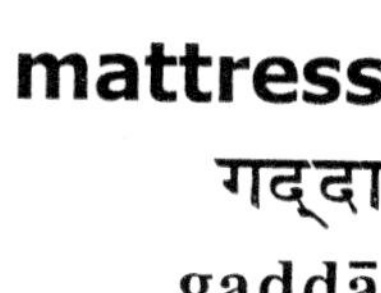

mattress
गद्दा
gaddā

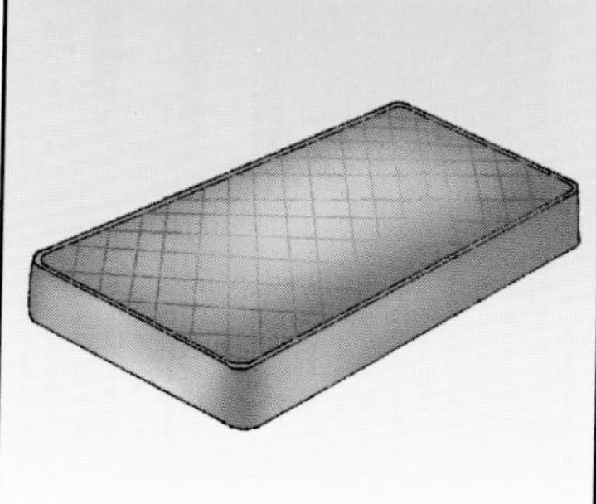

matchbox
माचिस
maachis

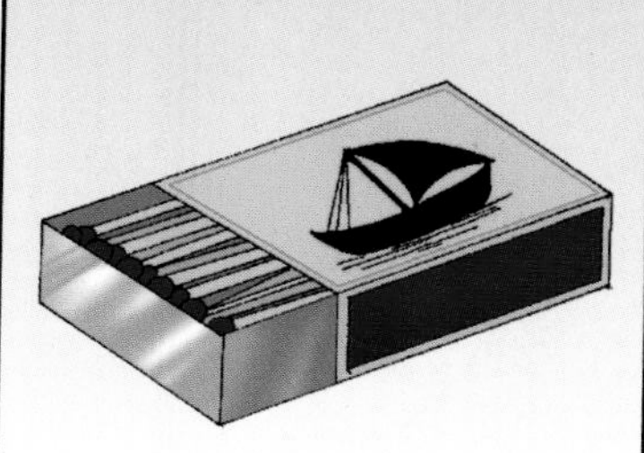

mop
झाड़ू
jhāḍū

necktie
टाई
tie

oven
तंदूर
tandūr

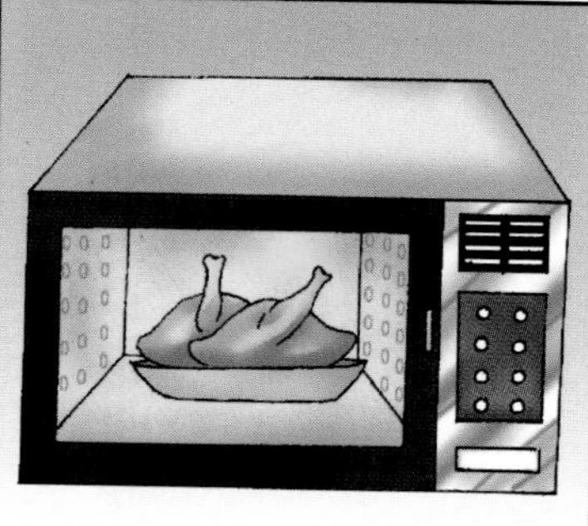

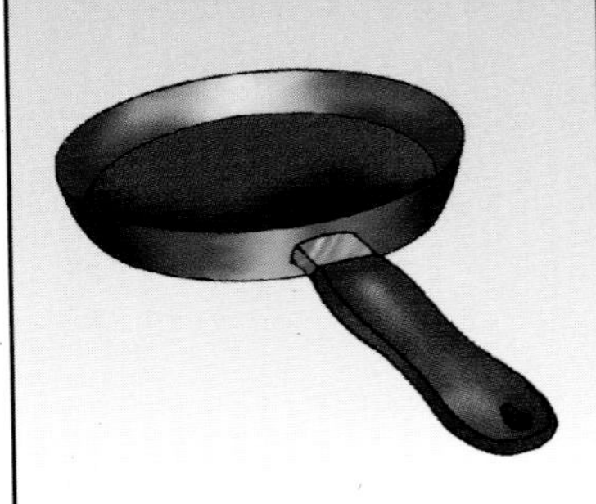

pan
तवा, कड़ाही
tava, kadahi

sewing machine
सिलाई मशीन
seelai mashin

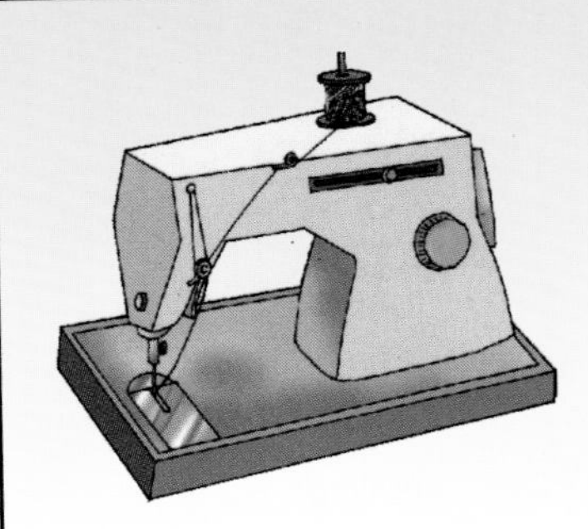

plate
थाली
thali

seats
आसन
āsan

pram
बच्चा गाड़ी
bacchā gādī

shelf
अलमारी का खाना
almārī ka khana

roof
छत
chhat

shower
बौछार
bauchhār

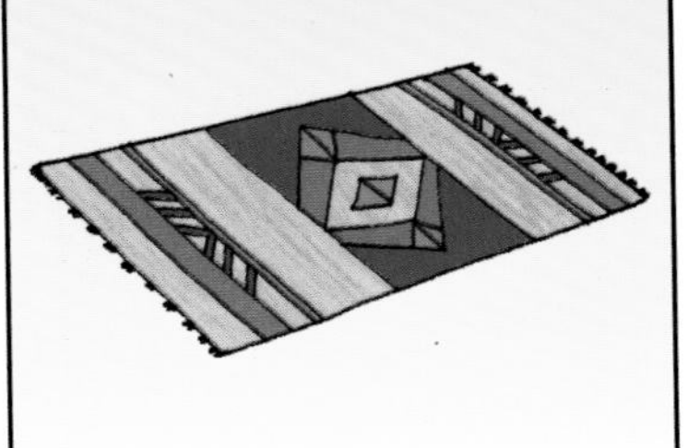

rug
कालीन
kālīn

sink
चिलमची
chilamchi

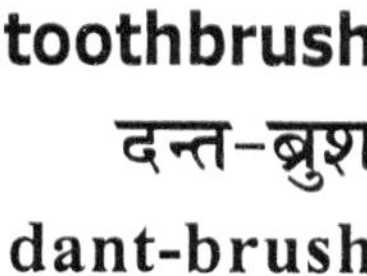

smoke
धुआँ
dhuān

sofa
सोफ़ा
sōfā

spanner
पाना
pana

stairs/ steps
सीढ़ियां
sīḍhiyān

toilet
शौचालय
shauchālaya

toothbrush
दन्त-ब्रुश
dant-brush

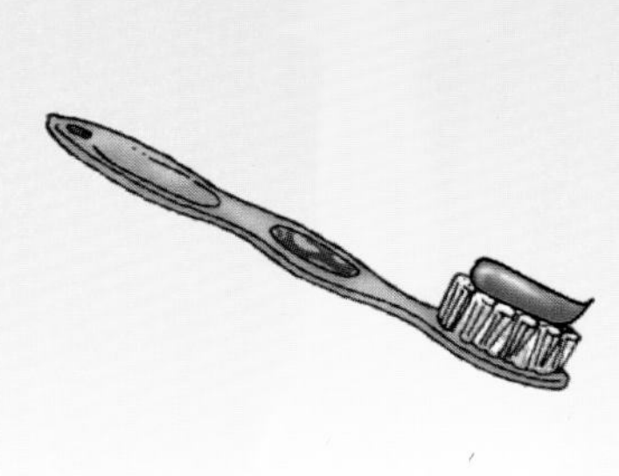

tub
स्नान टब
snān ṭab

wall
दीवार
dīvār

wardrobe
अलमारी
almārī

window
खिड़की
khiḍakī

bag
बस्ता
basta

clock
घड़ी
ghari

glass
ग्लास
glass

cushion
तकिया
takiyā

knife
चाकू
chāku

radio
रेडियो
radiyo

refrigerator
फ्रिज
frij

telephone
फोन
phone

stove
स्टोव
stove

table
मेज़
mez

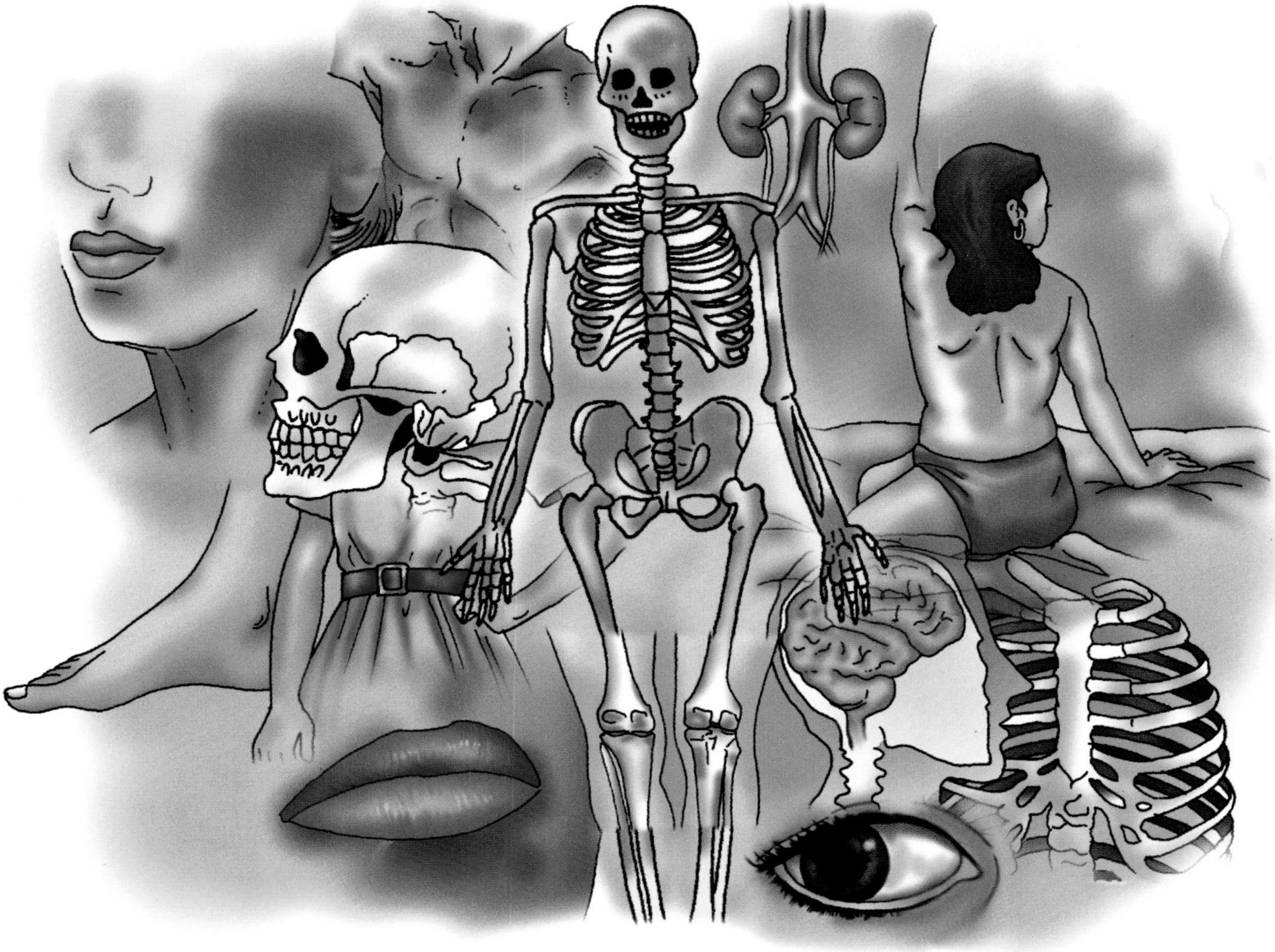

HUMAN BODY

मानव शरीर

mānav śarīr

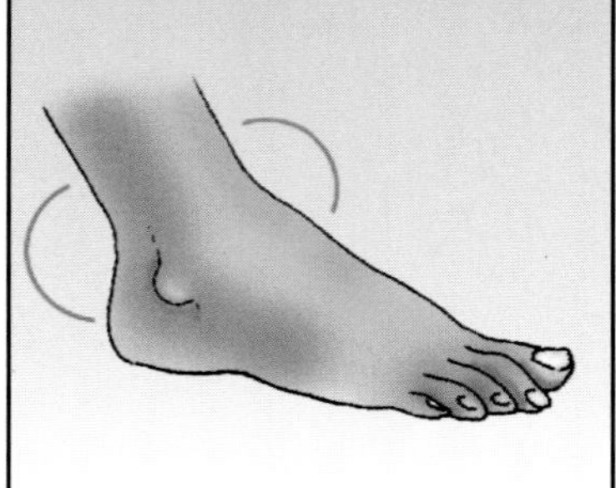

ankle
टखना
ṭakhanā

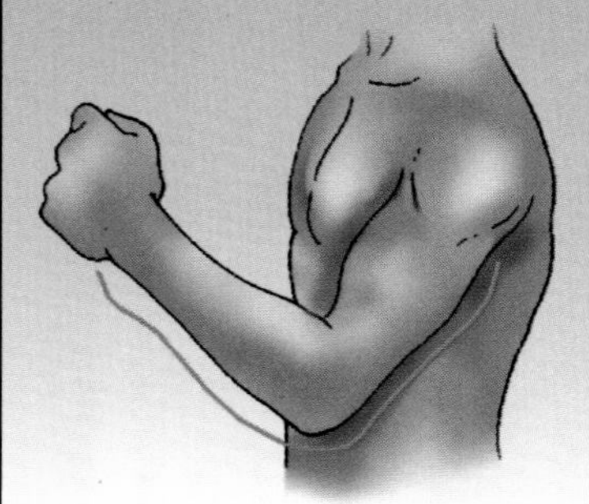

arm
बाँह
bānha

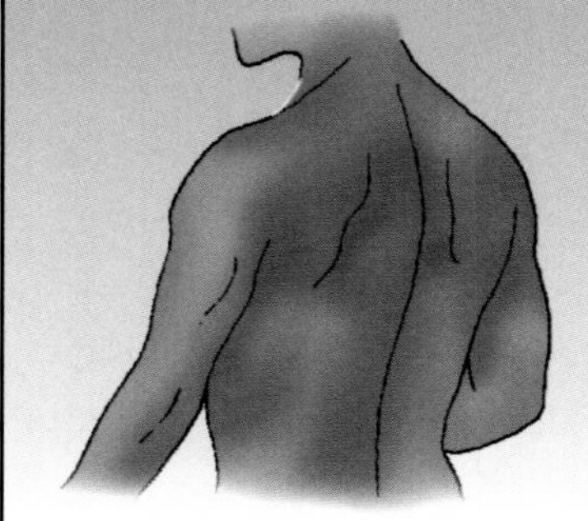

back
पीठ
peeth

beard
दाढ़ी
dādhi

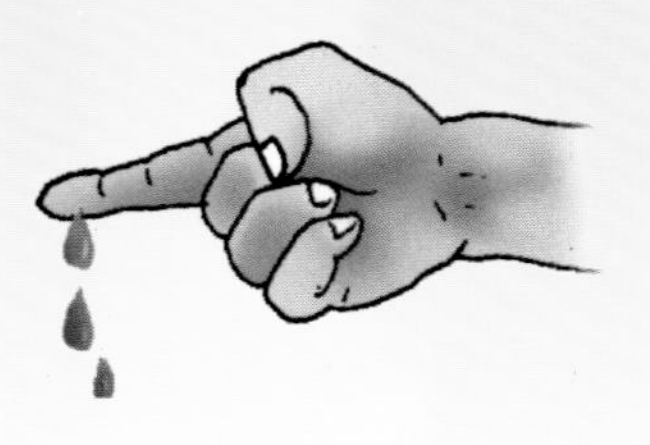

blood
खून,रक्त
khoon, rakt

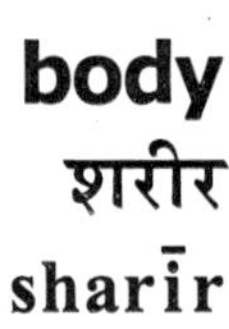

body
शरीर
sharīr

bone
हड्डी
haḍḍī

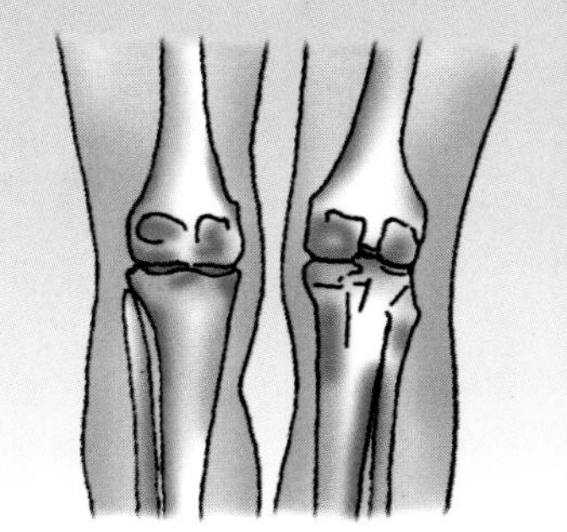

brain
मस्तिष्क
mastishk

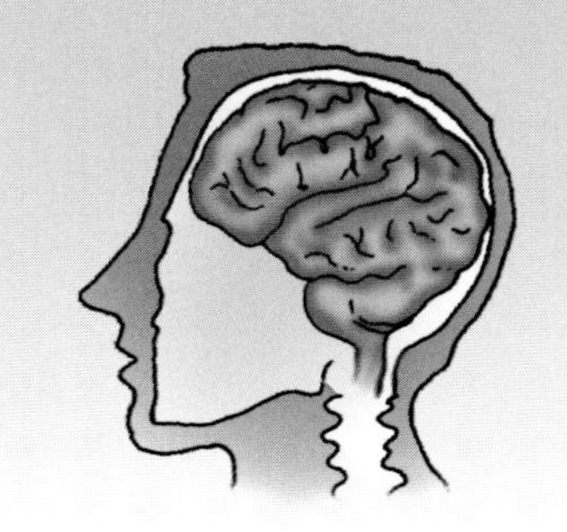

cheek
गाल
gaal

chest
छाती
chhātī

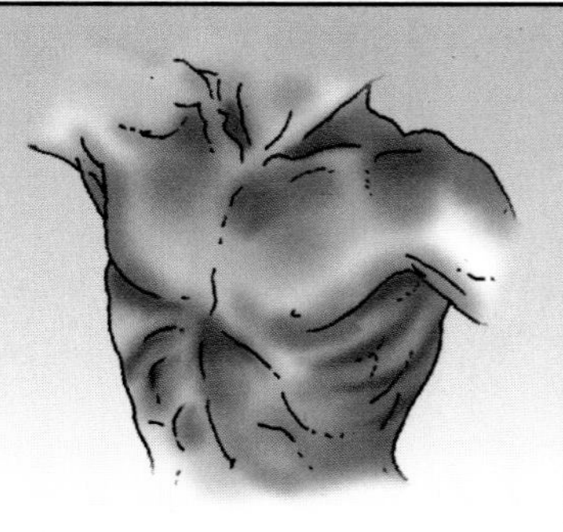

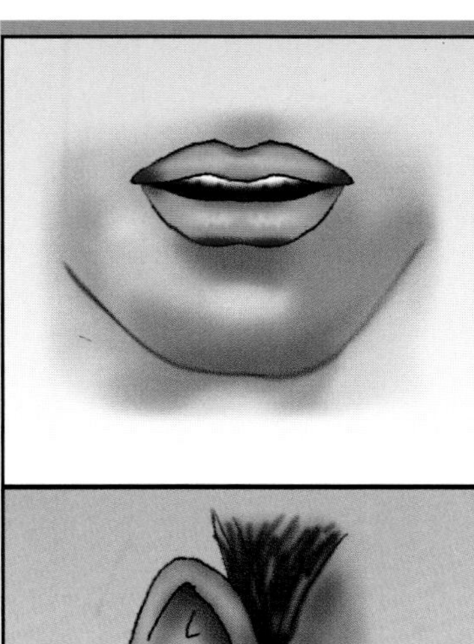

chin
ठोड़ी
thodi

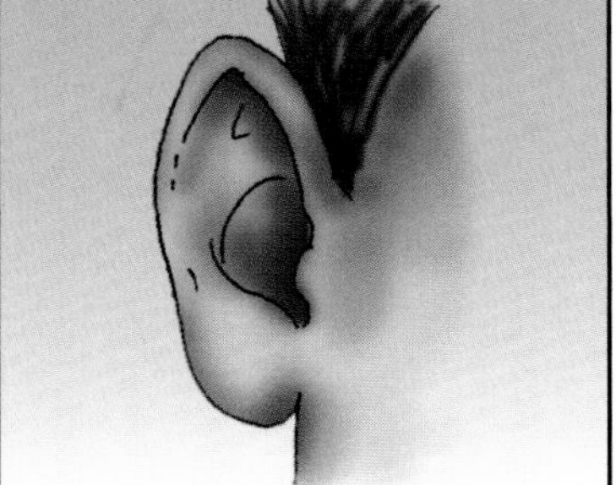

ear
कान
kaan

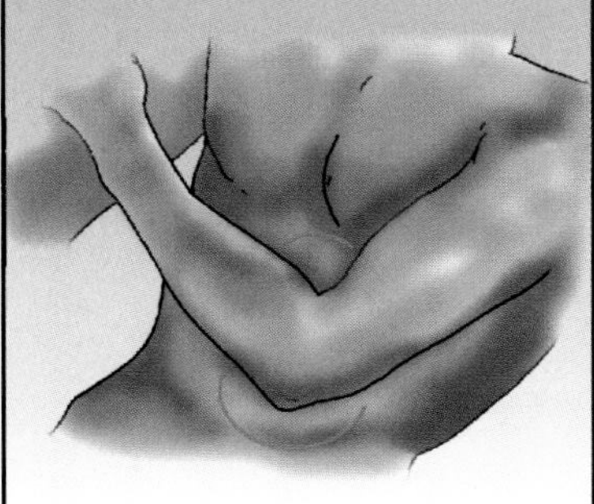

elbow
कोहनी
kōhanī

eye
आँख
ānkh

eyebrow
भौंह
bhonh

face
चेहरा
chēharā

finger
उँगली
ungali

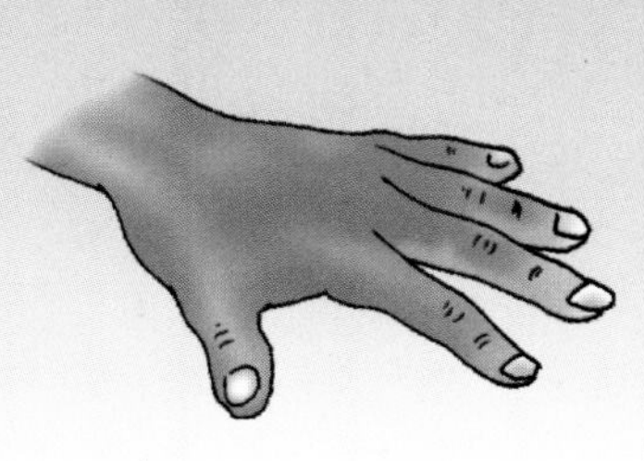

foot
पैर
pair

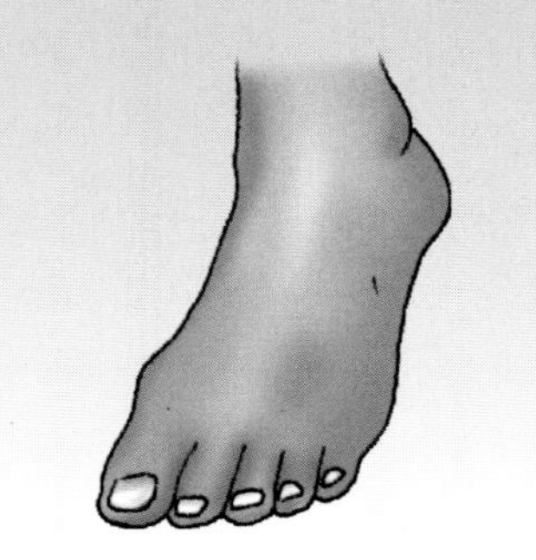

forehead
माथा
māthā

hair
बाल
baal

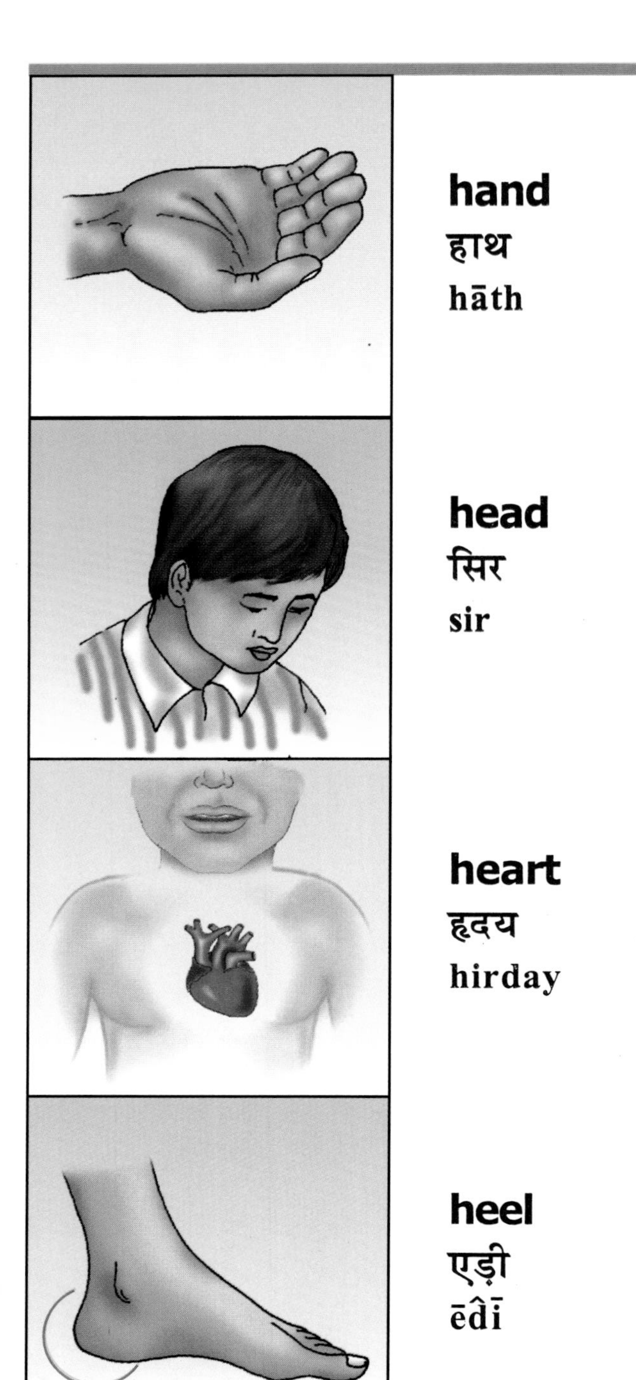

hand
हाथ
hāth

head
सिर
sir

heart
हृदय
hirday

heel
एड़ी
ēḍī

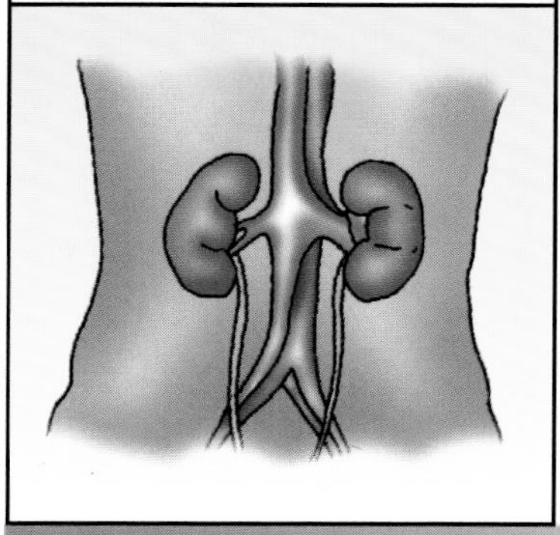

kidney
गुर्दा
gurdā

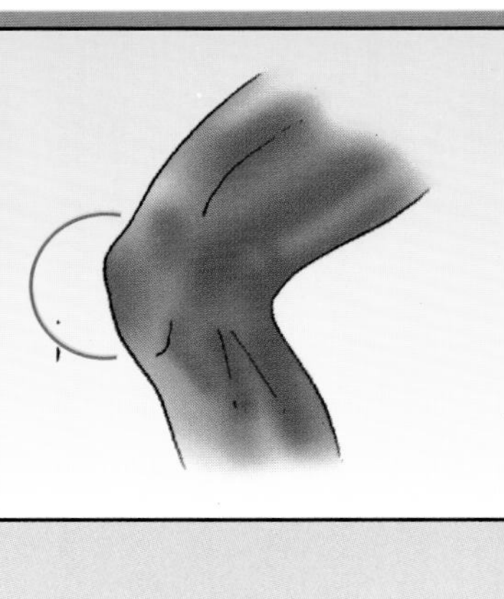

knee
घुटना
ghuṭanā

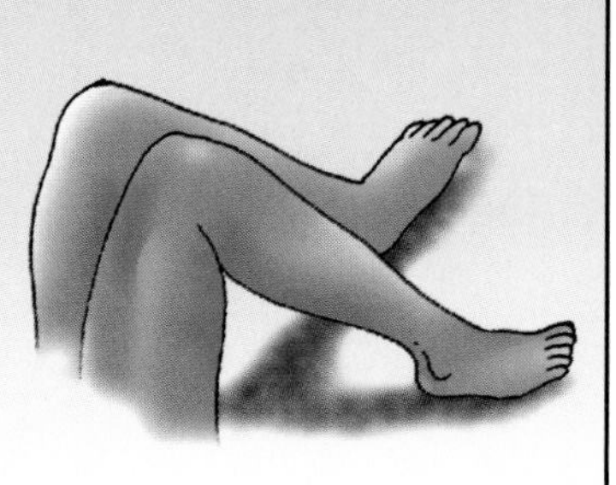

leg
टाँग
ṭāṅg

lips
होंठ
hōṇṭh

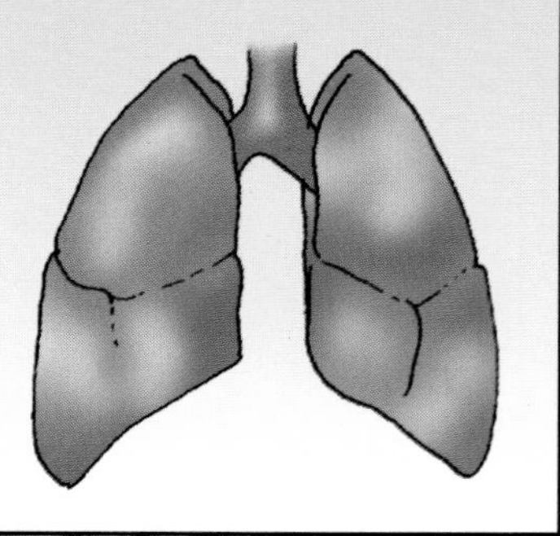

lungs
फेफड़े
phēphaḍē

mouth
मुख
mukh

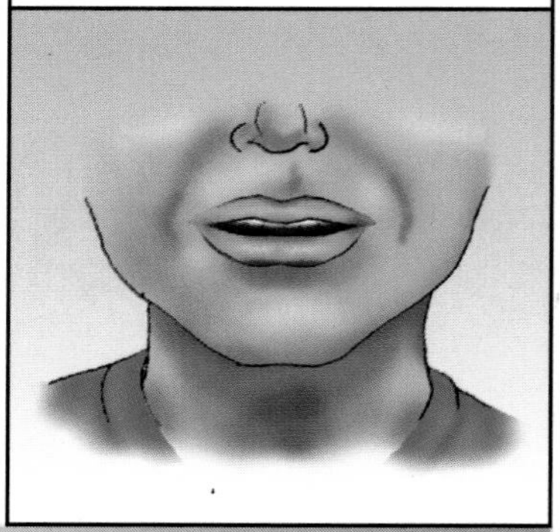

moustache
मूँछ
moonchh

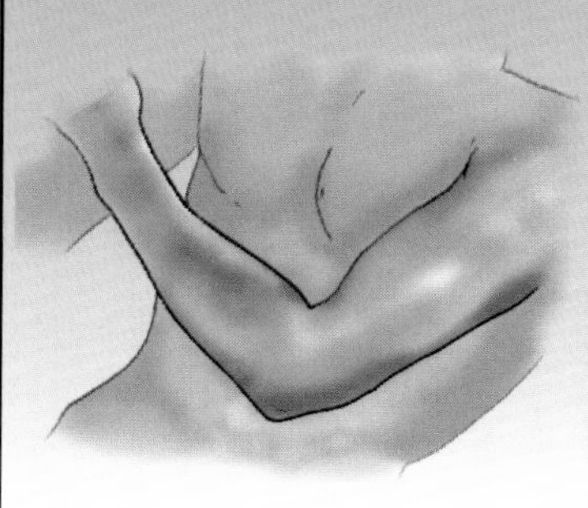

muscle
माँसपेशी
mānspeshi

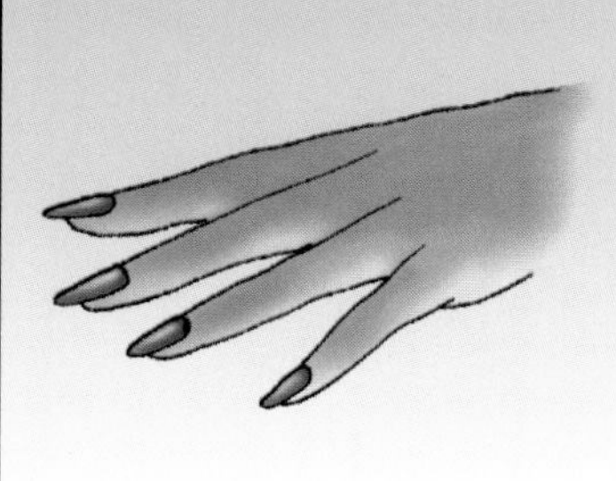

nails
नाखून
nākhūn

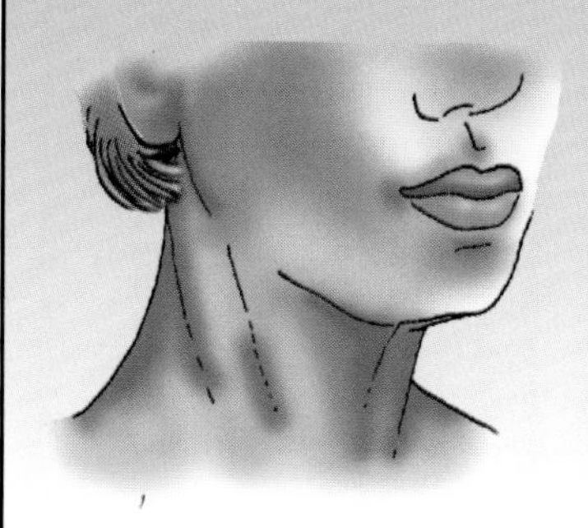

neck
गर्दन
gardan

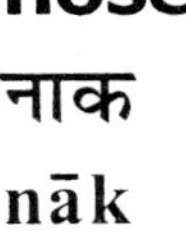

nose
नाक
nāk

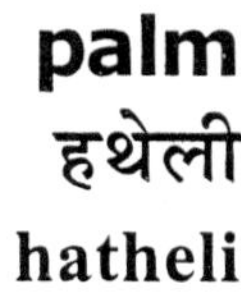

palm
हथेली
hatheli

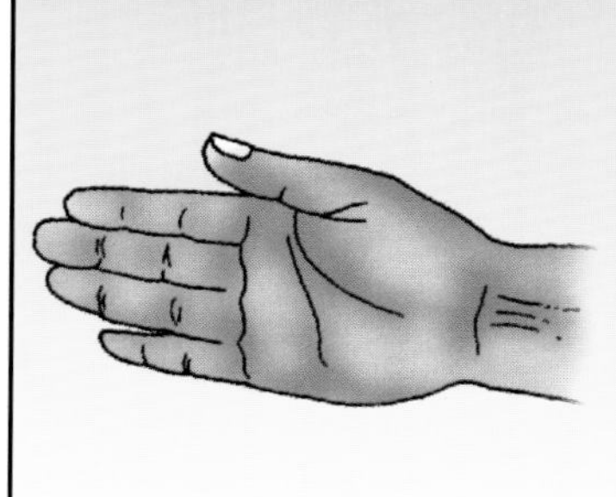

ribs
पसली
pasli

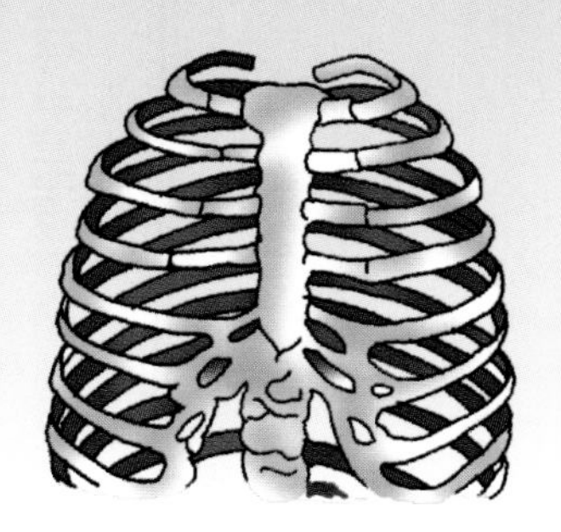

shoulder
कंधा
kandhā

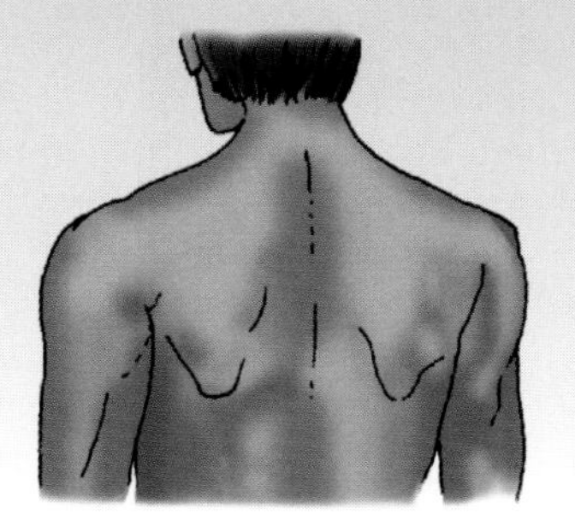

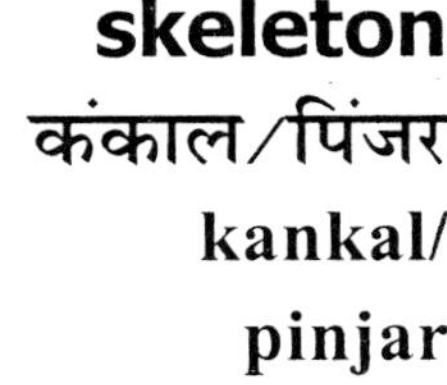

skeleton
कंकाल/पिंजर
kankal/
pinjar

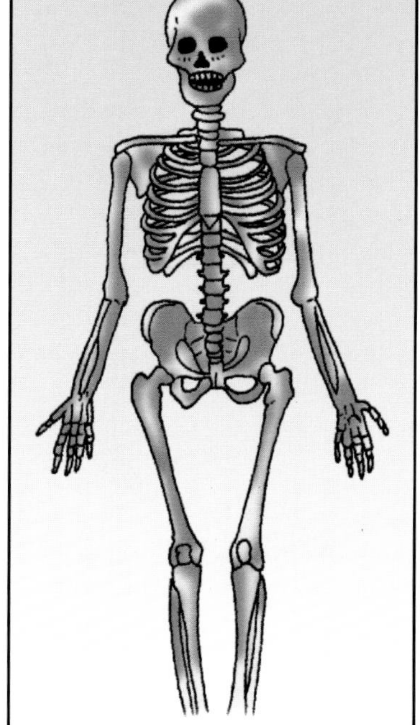

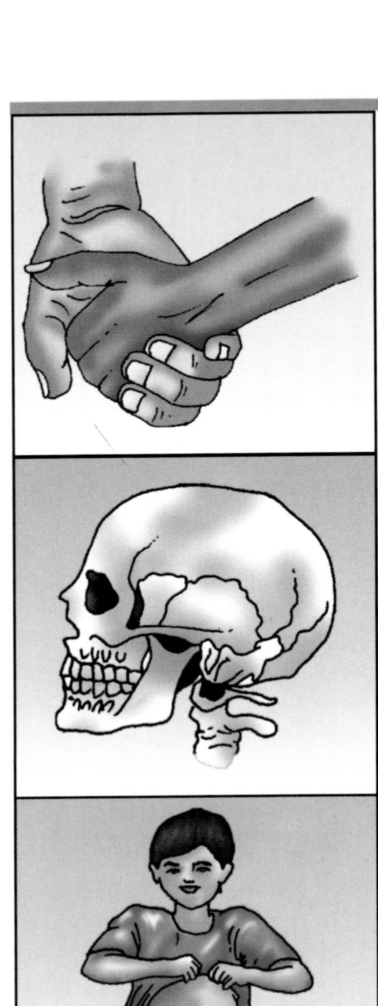

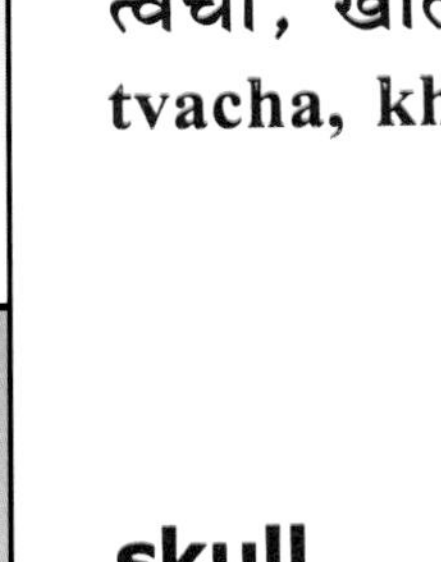

skin
त्वचा, खाल
tvacha, khaal

skull
खोपड़ी
khōpaḓī

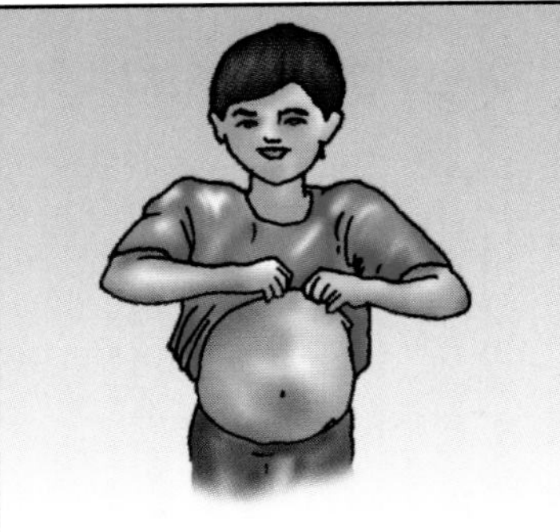

stomach
पेट
pēṭ

teeth
दाँत
dānt

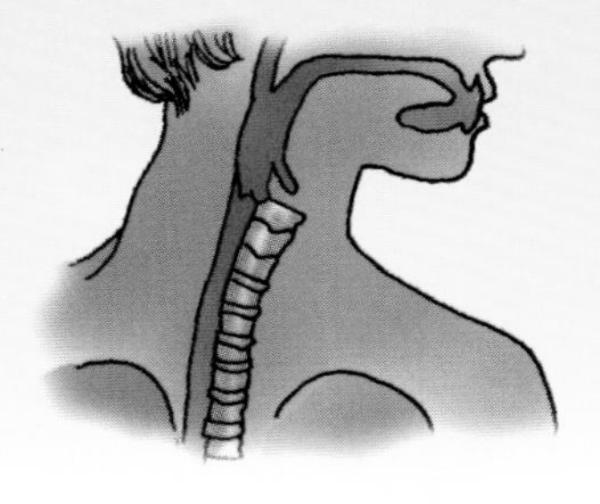

throat
गला
gala

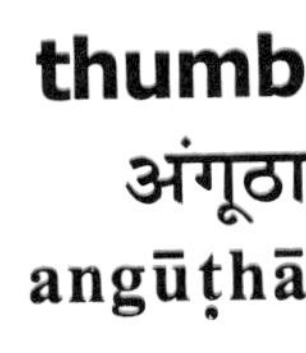

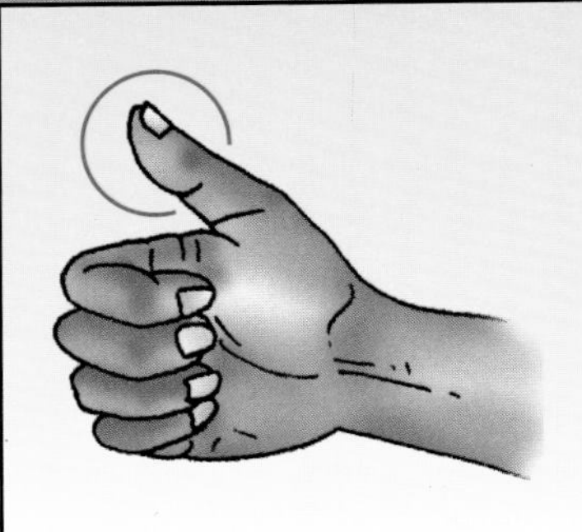

thumb
अंगूठा
angūṭhā

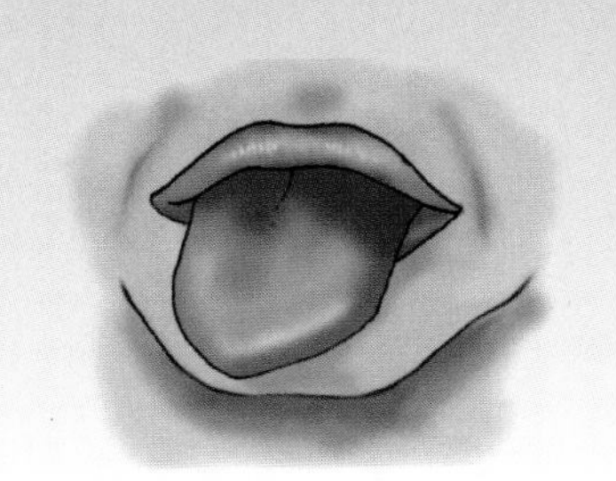

tongue
जीभ
jeebh

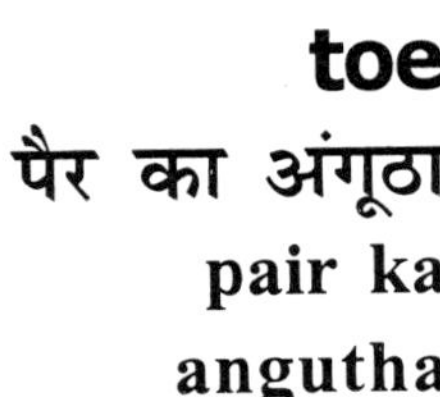

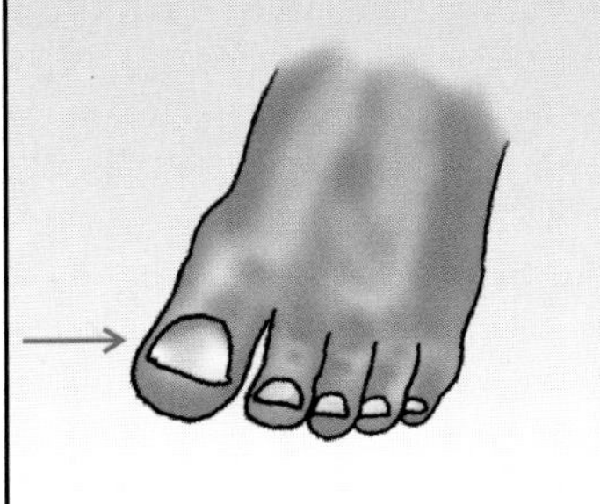

toe
पैर का अंगूठा
pair ka
angutha

waist
कमर
kamar

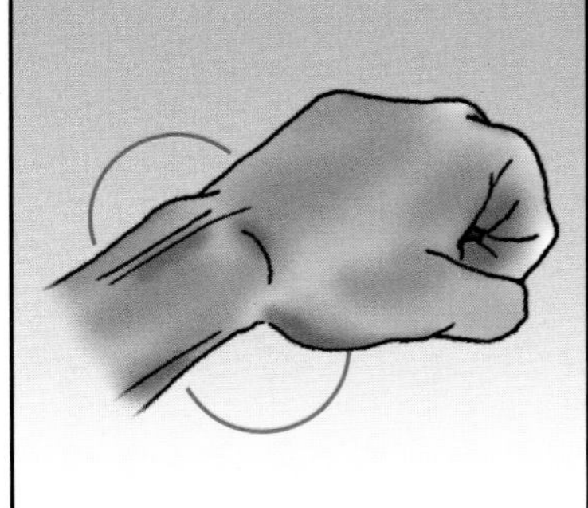

wrist
कलाई
kalāī

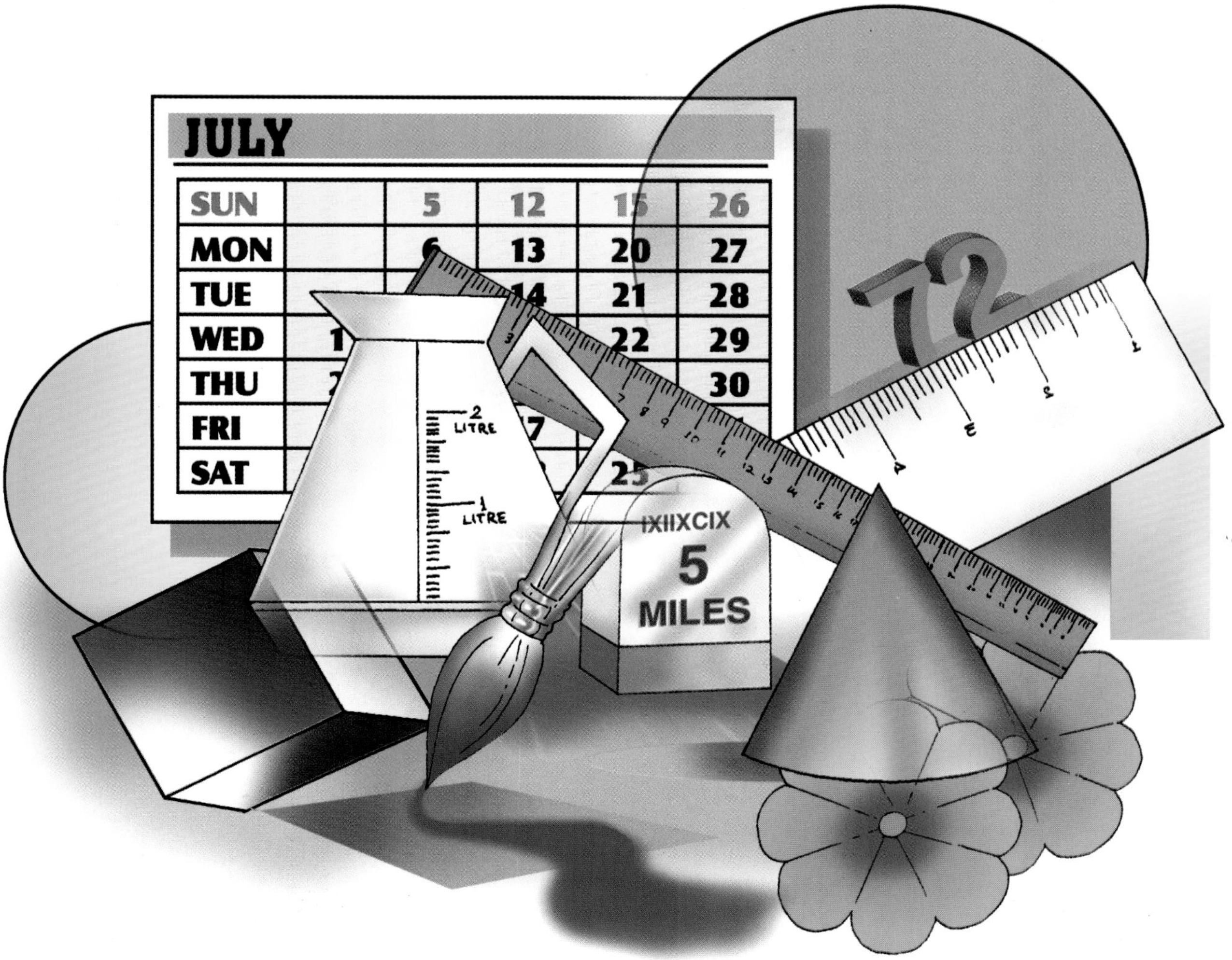

MEASUREMENTS, SHAPES, COLOURS AND TIME

माप तोल, आकार, रंग और समय

māp tōl, ākār, raṅg aur samay

black
काला
kālā

blue
नीला
nīlā

brown
भूरा
bhūrā

circle
गोलाकार
gōlākār

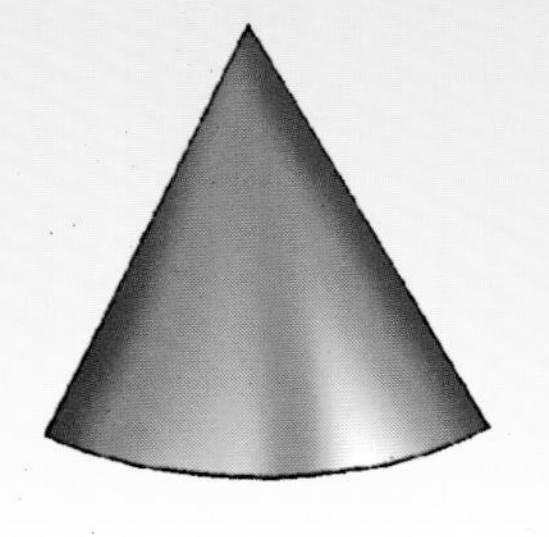

cone
शंकु
shaṅku

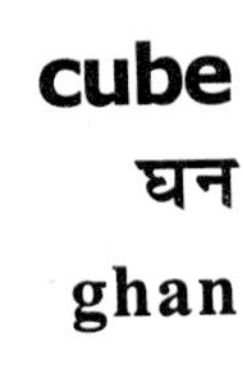

cube
घन
ghan

decimal
दशमलव
dashamlav

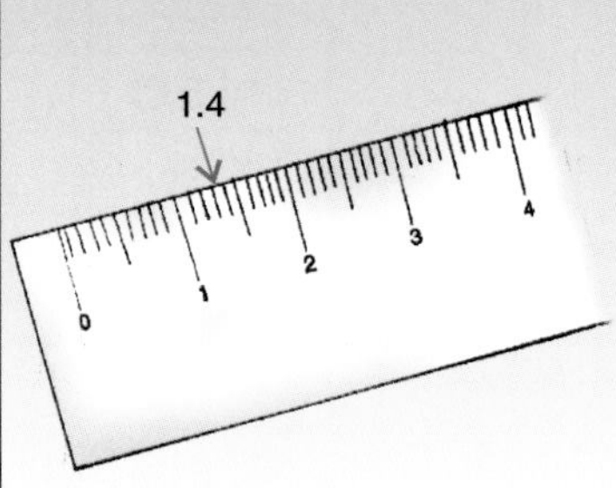

green
हरा
harā

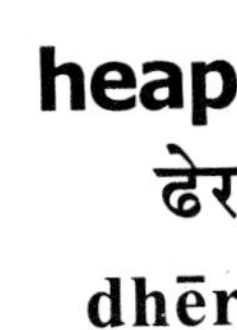

heap
ढेर
ḍhēr

kilogram
किलोग्राम
kilōgrām

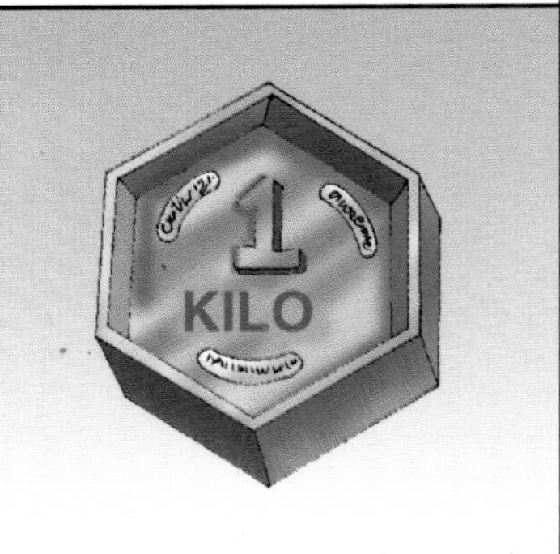

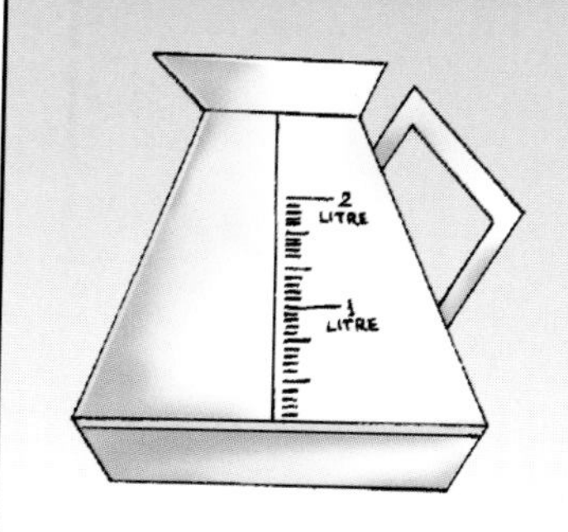

litre
लीटर
līṭar

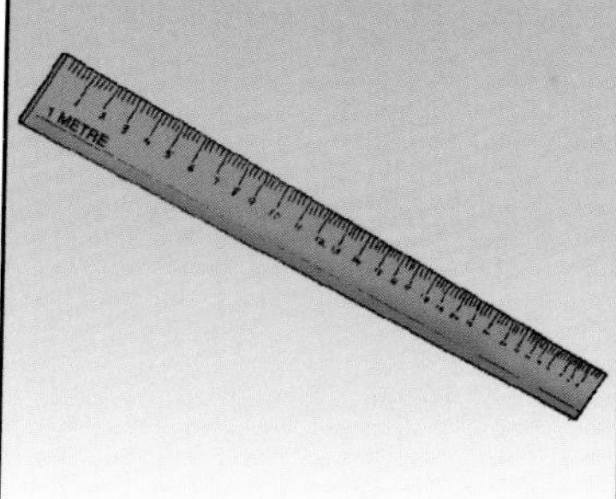

metre
मीटर
mīṭar

mile
मील
meel

8:25

minute
मिनट
minaṭ

JULY

SUN		5	12	15	26
MON		6	13	20	27
TUE		7	14	21	28
WED	1	8	15	22	29
THU	2	9	16	23	30
FRI	3	10	17	24	31
SAT	4	11	18	25	

month
महीना
mahīnā

oval
अंडाकार
anḍākār

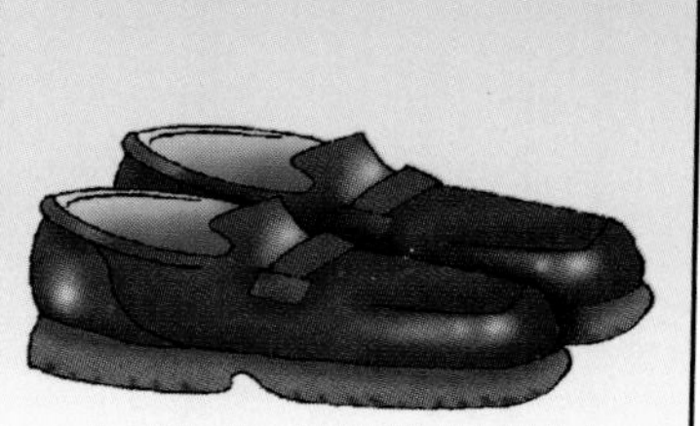

pair
जोड़ा
jōḍā

pink
गुलाबी
gulaabi

rectangle
आयत
āyat

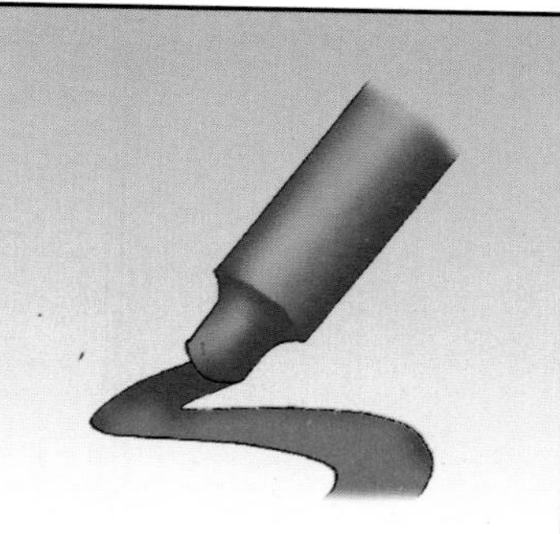

red
लाल
laal

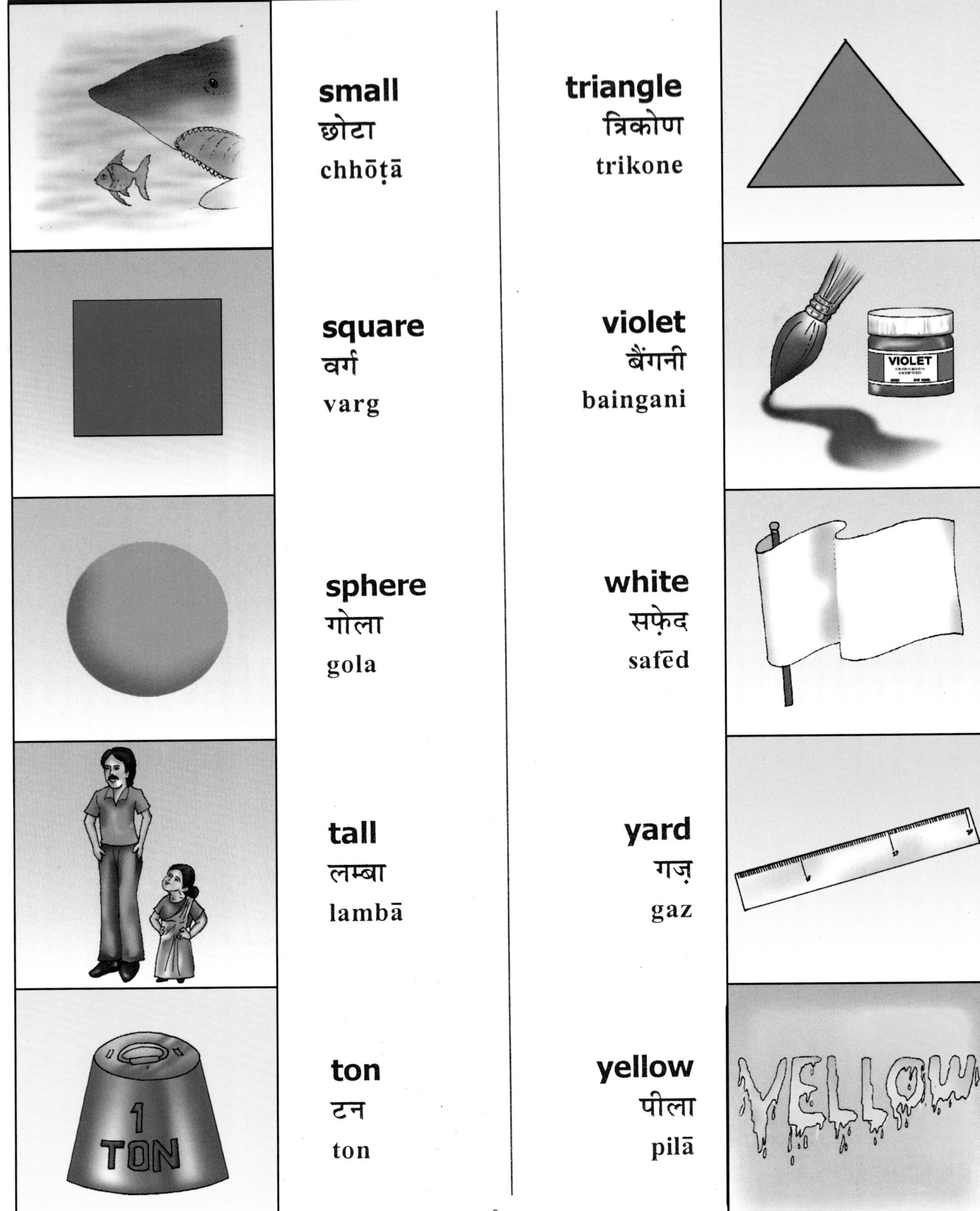
small
छोटा
chhōṭā
triangle
त्रिकोण
trikone
square
वर्ग
varg
violet
बैंगनी
baingani
VIOLET
sphere
गोला
gola
white
सफ़ेद
safēd
tall
लम्बा
lambā
yard
गज़
gaz
ton
टन
ton
1 TON
yellow
पीला
pilā
YELLOW

PEOPLE, COSTUMES AND ORNAMENTS

लोग, वेश-भूषा एवं अलंकार

lōg, vēś bhūṣhā ēvaṃ alankār

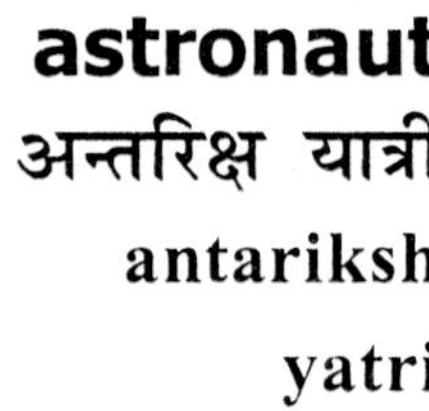

actor
अभिनेता
abhinētā

actress
अभिनेत्री
abhinētrī

angel
फरिश्ता
farishta

architect
शिल्पकार
shilpkār

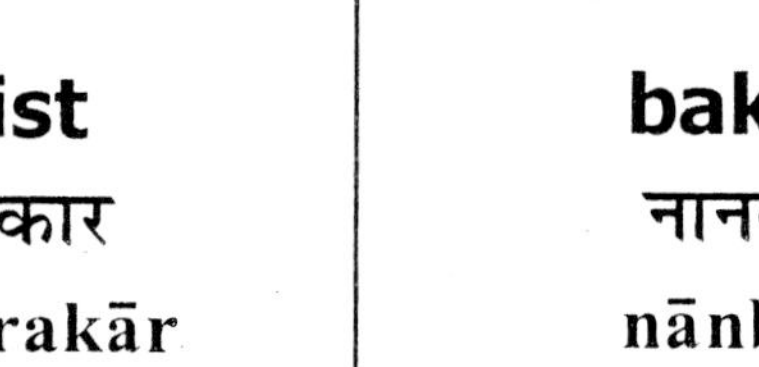

artist
चित्रकार
chitrakār

astronaut
अन्तरिक्ष यात्री
antariksh
yatri

athlete
खिलाड़ी
khilāḍī

author
लेखक
lēkhak

baby
छोटा बच्चा
chhōṭā
bacchā

baker
नानबाई
nānbāī

bandit
डाकू
ḍākū

bride
दुल्हन
dūlhan

bishop
पादरी
pādarī

bridegroom
दूल्हा
dūlhā

blacksmith
लुहार
luhār

captain
कप्तान
kaptān

blouse
ब्लाउज
blouse

cap
टोपी
topi

boy
लड़का
laḍakā

carpenter
बढ़ई
baḍhaī

child
बच्चा
bacchā

clown
जोकर
jōkar

conductor
परिचालक
parichālak

cook/chef
रसोइया
rasōiyā

dancers
नर्तक
nartak

daughter
बेटी
bēṭi

dentist
दन्त चिकित्सक
dant
chikitsak

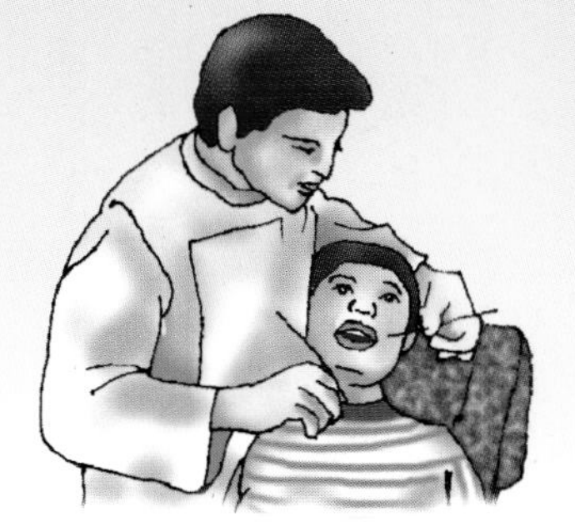

doctor
चिकित्सक
chikitsak

driver
चालक
chālak

dwarf
बौना
bauna

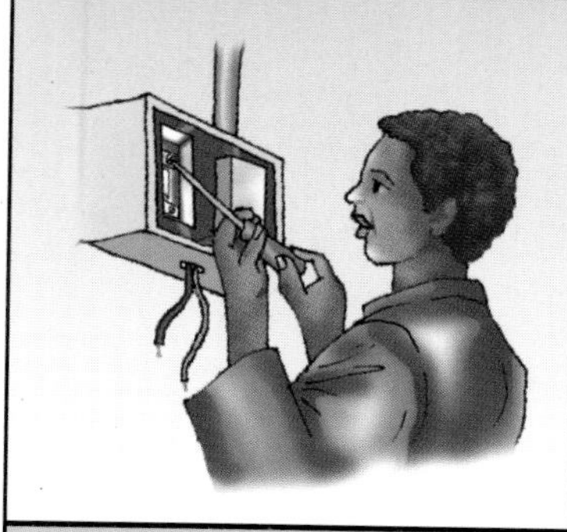

electrician
बिजली मिस्त्री
bijalī mistrī

farmer
किसान
kisān

fire-fighter
अग्नि शामक
agni shāmak

girl
लड़की
laḍakī

jacket
जैकेट
jacket

king
राजा
rājā

knight
शूरवीर
shoorvīr

lady
महिला
mahilā

man
आदमी
ādmī

mechanic
मिस्त्री
mistrī

miner
खनिक
khanik

merchant
व्यापारी
vyāpārī

monk
भिक्षुक
bhikshuk

musician
संगीतकार
saṅgītkār

necktie
टाई
tie

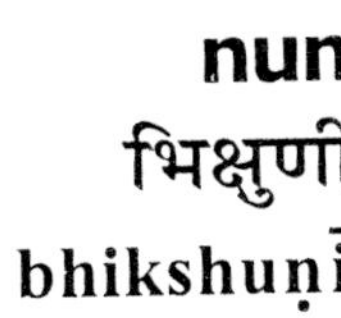

nun
भिक्षुणी
bhikshuṇī

nurse
परिचारिका
parichārikā

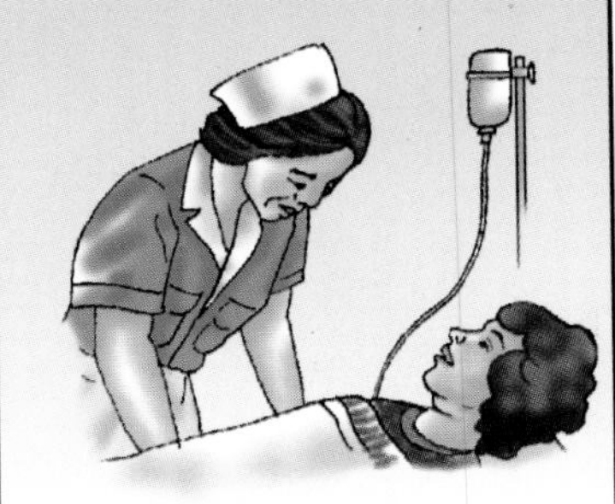

painter
रंगसाज
rangsaj

pilot
विमान चालक
vimān chālak

plumber
नल मिस्त्री
nal mistrī

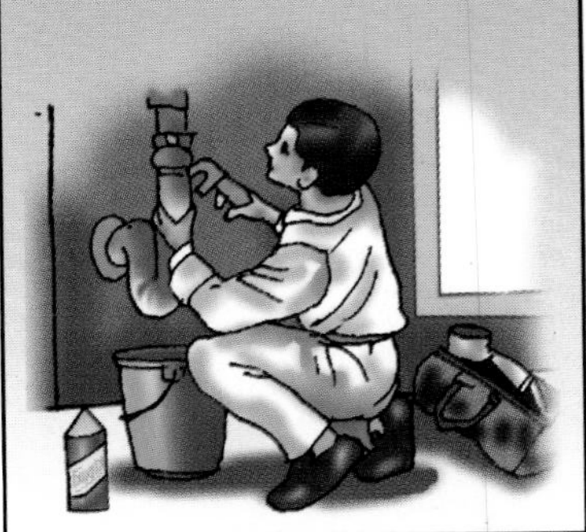

police officer
पुलिस अधिकारी
police adhikari

porter
कुली
kulī

postman
डाकिया
ḍākiyā

priest
पुजारी
pujārī

prince
राजकुमार
rājkumār

queen
रानी
rānī

robber
लुटेरा
luṭēra

sailor
नाविक
navik

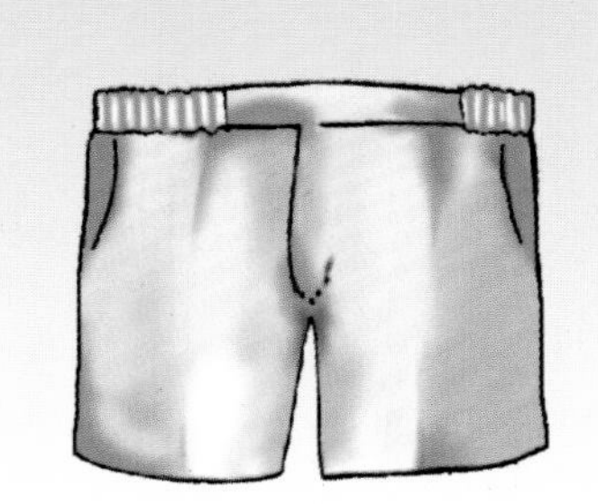

shorts
निक्कर
nikkar

shopkeeper
दुकानदार
dukāndār

sisters
बहनें
bahanēn

soldier
सैनिक
sainik

solicitor
वकील
vakīl

teacher
शिक्षक
shikshak

thief
चोर
chor

turban
पगड़ी
pagri

waiter
बैरा
bera

wife
पत्नी
patnī

woman
स्त्री
strī

wrestlers
पहलवान
pahalvān

PLACES AND BUILDINGS

स्थान एवं भवन

sthān ēvaṃ bhavan

airport
हवाई अड्डा
hawai adda

aquarium
मत्स्यालय
matsyalay

bank
बैंक
bank

bay
खाड़ी
khāḍī

bazaar
बाज़ार
bāzār

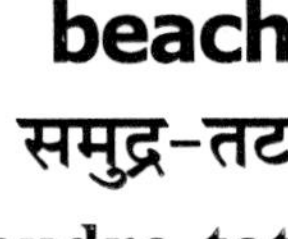

beach
समुद्र-तट
samudra-taṭ

bridge
पुल
pul

bungalow
बंगला
bangla

café
कॉफी हाउस
kāfi hāus

canal
नहर
nahar

castle
दुर्ग
durg

cathedral
मुख्य गिरजाघर
mukhya
girjāghar

cave
गुफ़ा
gufa

church
गिरजाघर
girjāghar

cinema
सिनेमा
sinema

circus
सर्कस
sarkas

clinic
छोटा अस्पताल
chhōṭā aspatāl

coast
समुद्र तट
samudra-taṭ

college
महाविद्यालय
mahāvidyālaya

cottage
कुटिया
kutiya

court
न्यायालय
nyāyālay

farm
खेत
khēt

den
माँद
mānd

apartment
फ्लैट
flat

desert
रेगिस्तान
rēgistān

forest
जंगल
jangal

dome
गुम्बद
gumbad

fort
किला
kilā

factory
कारखाना
kārkhānā

gallery
दीर्घा
dīrghā

petrol station
पैट्रोल पम्प
paiṭrōl pump

garden
बाग़
bāgh

glacier
हिमनदी
himnadi

gulf
खाड़ी
khāḍī

hill
पहाड़
pahad

hospital
अस्पताल
aspatāl

hostel
छात्रावास
chhātrāvās

hotel
होटल
hōṭal

house
मकान
makān

hut
झोंपड़ी
jhonpadi

inn
सराय
sarāi

island
द्वीप
dvīp

laboratory
प्रयोगशाला
prayōgshālā

lake
झील
jheel

lane
गली
gali

library
पुस्तकालय
pustakālaya

light house
प्रकाश स्तम्भ
prakāsh stambh

market
बाज़ार
bāzār

monument
स्मारक
smarak

mosque
मस्जिद
masjid

mountain
पर्वत
parvat

museum
संग्रहालय
saṅgrahālay

observatory
वेधशाला
vēdhshālā

ocean
महासागर
mahāsāgar

office
कार्यालय
kāryālay

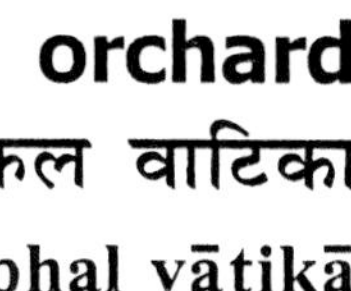

orchard
फल वाटिका
phal vāṭikā

palace
महल
mahal

park
बगीचा
bagīchā

pavement
पटरी
paṭrī

pillars
खम्भे
khambhē

play ground
खेल मैदान
khēl maidān

pond
तालाब
tālāb

pool
ताल
tāl

port
बंदरगाह
bandargāh

post-office
डाकखाना
dākkhānā

prison
जेल
jēl

restaurant
जलपान गृह
jalpān grih

river
नदी
nadī

road
सड़क
sad̂ak

school
विद्यालय
vidyālay

workshop
कारखाना
karkhānā

shop
दुकान
dukān

skyscraper
गगनचुम्बी
इमारत
gaganchumbī
imārat

stadium
स्टेडियम
sṭēḍiyam

station
स्टेशन
sṭēshan

street
गली
galī

subway
सुरंग पथ
surang path

supermarket
बड़ा बाज़ार
baḍā bāzār

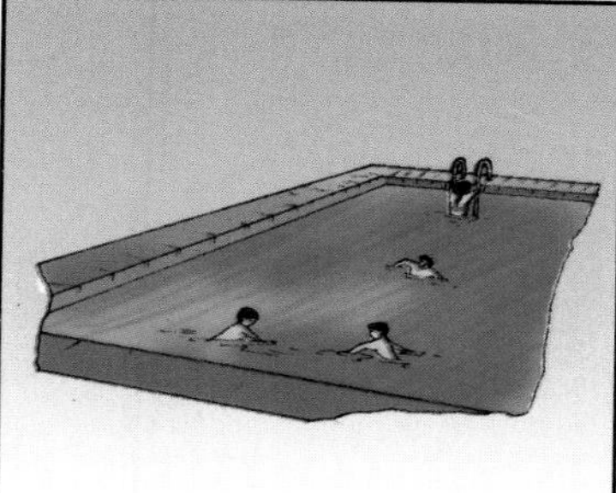

swimming pool
तरणताल
taraṇ tāl

temple
मंदिर
mandir

theatre
रंगशाला
raṅgshālā

tower
मीनार
mīnār

town
नगर
nagar

tunnel
सुरंग
suraṅg

university
विश्वविद्यालय
vishvavidyālay

valley
घाटी
ghāti

village
गाँव
gānv

ward/clinic
चिकित्सालय
chikitsalay

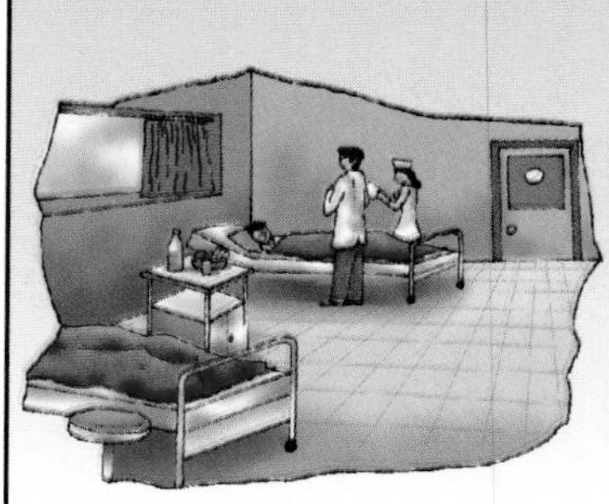

zoo
चिड़ियाघर
chiriyaghar

PLANTS AND FLOWERS

पौधे और फूल

paudhē aur phūl

balsam
गुल मेहँदी
gul
mēhandī

bamboo
बाँस
bāns

branch
टहनी
ṭahanī

bush
झाड़ी
jhāḍī

cactus
कैक्टस
kaikṭas

corn
मक्का
makkā

cotton
कपास
kapās

daffodil
पीला नरगिस
pīlā nargis

dandelion
डंडेलियन
ḍaṇḍēliyan

eggplant
बैंगन
baiṅgan

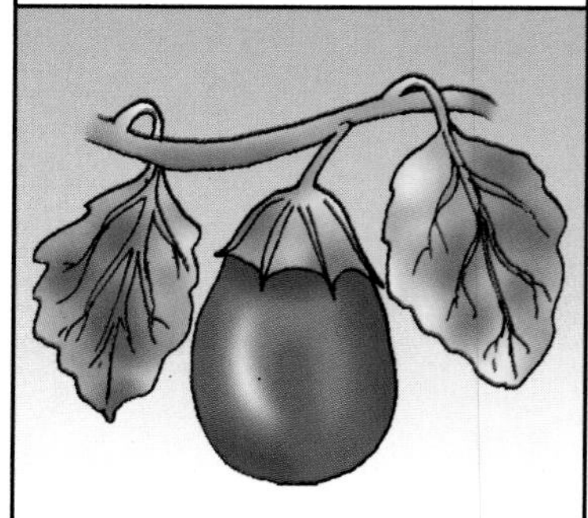

elm
चिराबेल
chirābēl

fir
देवदार
dēvdār

flax
सन
san

grass
घास
ghās

heliopsis
सूर्य कमल
sūrya kamal

honey-suckle
तिन पत्तिया
tin pattiyā

jasmine
चमेली
chamēlī

lily

कुमुदिनी
kumudinī

maize
मक्का
makkā

narcissus
नरगिस
nargis

olive
जैतून
zaitūn

palm trees
ताड़
tād̂

peas
मटर
maṭar

root
जड़
jad̂

rose
गुलाब
gulāb

sugarcane
गन्ना
gannā

tobacco
तंबाकू
tambāku

vanilla
वैनिला
vainilā

water-lily
कमलिनी
kamaleeni

zinnias
ज़ीनियास
zinnias

SPORTS, GAMES AND RECREATION

खेल, कूद एवं मनोरंजन

khēl, kūd ēvaṃ manōrañjan

arrow
तीर
tīr

archery
धनुर्विद्या
dhanurvidya

badminton
बैडमिंटन
baiḍmiṇṭan

ball
गेंद
gaind

balloon
गुब्बारा
gubbārā

billiard
बिलियर्ड
biliyarḍ

carrom board
कैरम बोर्ड
kairam bōrḍ

chess
शतरंज
shatrañj

clarinet
शहनाई
shahnāi

cornet
नगाड़ा
nagāḍā

drum
ढोल
ḍhōl

flute
बाँसुरी
bānsurī

cricket
क्रिकेट
krikēṭ

football
फुटबाल
phuṭbāl

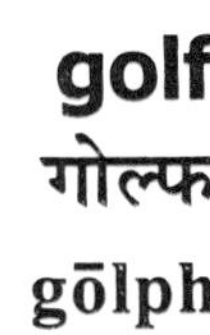

golf
गोल्फ
gōlph

guitar
गिटार
giṭār

hockey
हॉकी
hockey

kite
पतंग
pataṅg

mandolin
वीणा
vīṇā

puppets
कठपुतली
kaṭhputlī

racket
रैकेट
raikēṭ

seesaw
सी-सा
sī-sô

shuttle-cock
शॅटल कॉक
shaiṭal kôk

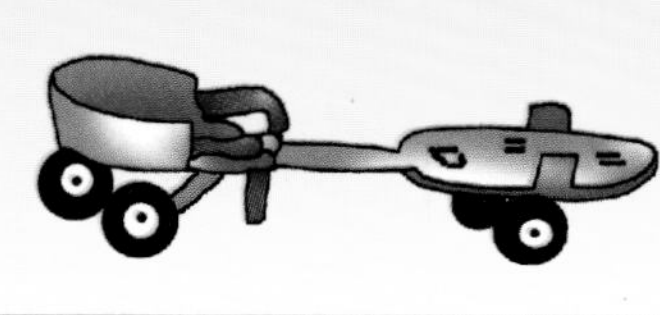

skates
पहिएदार जूता
pahiēdār
jūtā

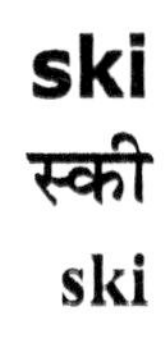

ski
स्की
ski

swing
झूला
jhūlā

tennis
टैनिस
tennis

trumpet
बिगुल
bigul

violin
वायलन
vayalan

TRANSPORT AND COMMUNICATION

परिवहन एवं संचार

parivahan evam sañchār

aeroplane
वायुयान
vāyuyān

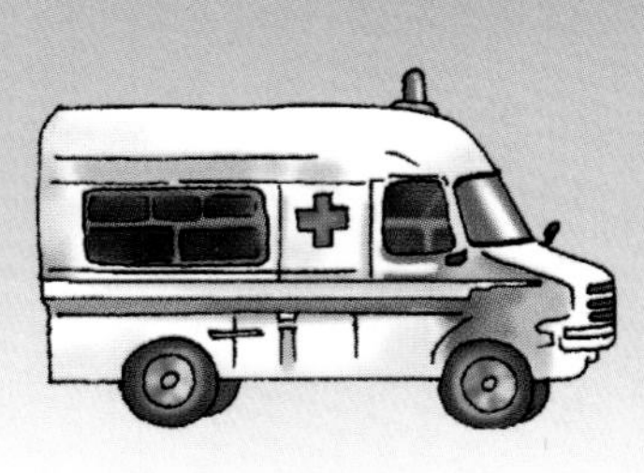

ambulance
रोगी-यान
rōgī-yān

automobile
मोटर गाड़ी
mōṭar gāḍī

balloon
गुब्बारा
gubbārā

bicycle
साईकल
sāikil

boat
नौका
naukā

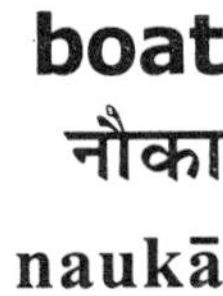

bus
बस
bas

bullock cart
बैल गाड़ी
bail gāḍī

bull-dozer
बुलडोजर
buldozer

cable car
केबल कार
kable kār

car
कार
kār

caravan
बन्द गाड़ी
band gādī

cart
हाथ ठेला
hāth ṭhēlā

chariot
रथ
rath

coach
सवारी बस
savārī bas

crane
क्रेन
krēn

double decker bus
बस
bus

engine (railway)
रेल इंजन
rail injan

fax
फैक्स मशीन
phaiks mashīn

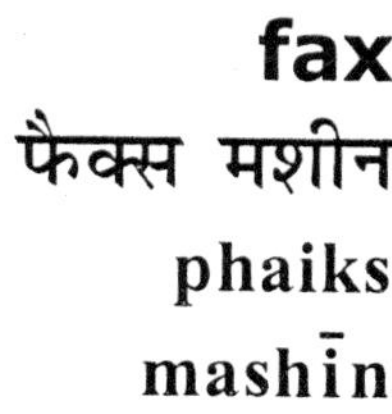

fire-engine
अग्नि इंजन
agni injan

generator
जेनरेटर
jēnarēṭar

motorcycle
मोटर साईकिल
mōṭar sāīkil

helicopter
हैलीकॉप्टर
hailīkāpṭar

parachute
हवाई छतरी
havāī chhatarī

hover-craft
तेज़ मशीनी नौका
tēz mashīnī naukā

petrol pump
पैट्रोल पम्प
paiṭrōl pump

jeep
जीप
jīp

post-card
पोस्ट कार्ड
pōsṭ kārḍ

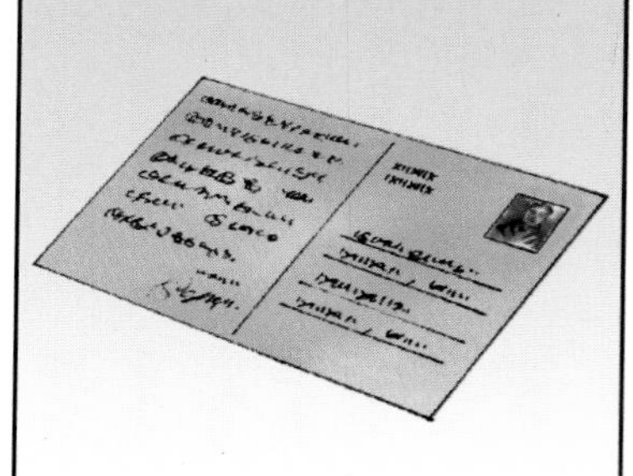

letter
पत्र
patr

radio
रेडियो
rēḍiyō

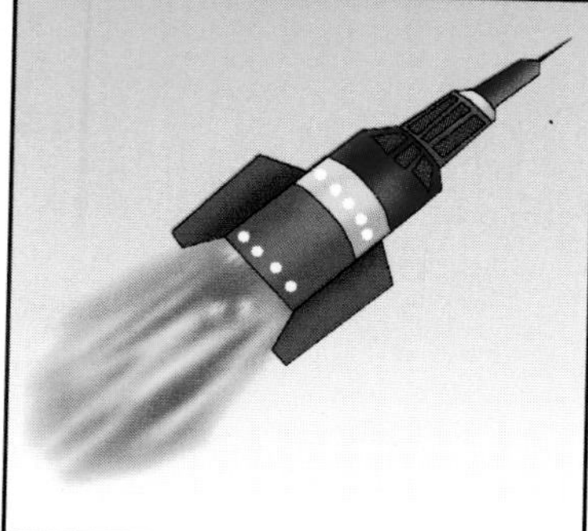

rocket
रोकेट
rocket

scooter
स्कूटर
skūṭar

ship
जलयान, जहाज
jalayān, jahaj

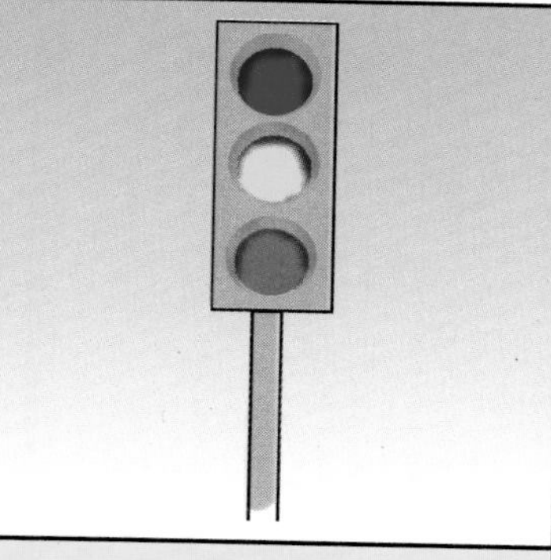

signal
संकेत
saṅkēt

stamp
डाक-टिकट
dāk-ṭikaṭ

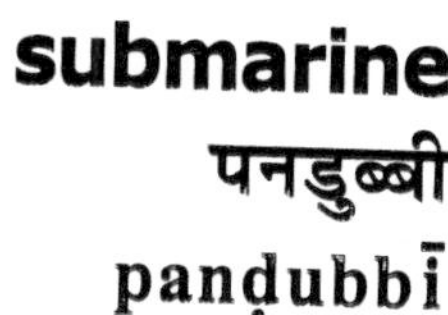

submarine
पनडुब्बी
panḍubbī

tanker
टैंकर
tankar

taxi
टैक्सी
taxi

telephone
दूरभाष
doorbhāsh

television
टेलीविज़न
ṭēlivision

typewriter
टाईपराइटर
typeritar

tractor
ट्रैक्टर
tractor

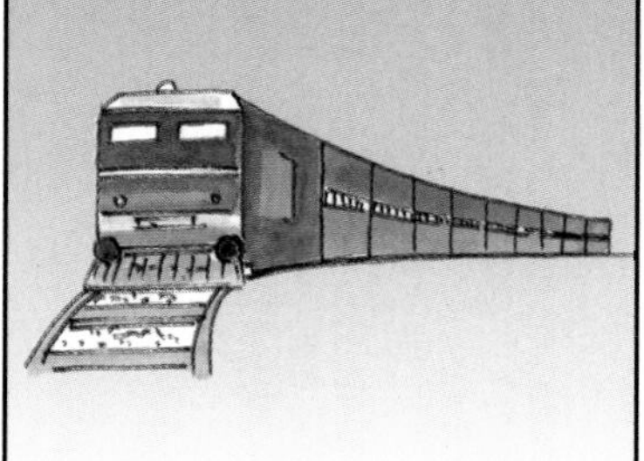

train
रेल गाड़ी
railgaṛi

tricycle
ट्राईसाइकिल
trisāīkil

tri-rikshaw
रिक्शा
rickshāw

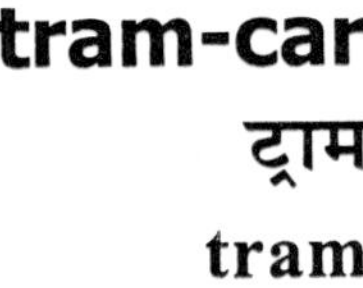

tram-car
ट्राम
tram

van
बन्द गाड़ी
band gaṛi

vehicles
वाहन
vāhan

wheel
पहिया
pahiyā

yacht
पाल वाली नौका
pāl vālī naukā

UNIVERSE AND WEATHER
सृष्टि एवं मौसम
sṛṣṭi ēvaṃ mausam

atom
परमाणु
parmāṇu

autumn
शरद् ऋतु
sharad ritu

avalanche
हिमधाव
himdhāv

blizzard
बर्फीला तूफान
barphīlā tūphān

cloud
बादल
bādal

comet

धूमकेतू
dhūmkētū

drought
सूखा
sūkhā

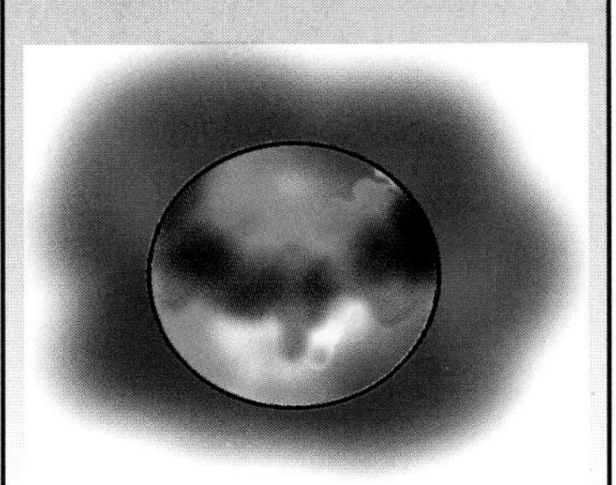

earth
पृथ्वी
pṛthvī

earthquake
भूकम्प
bhūkamp

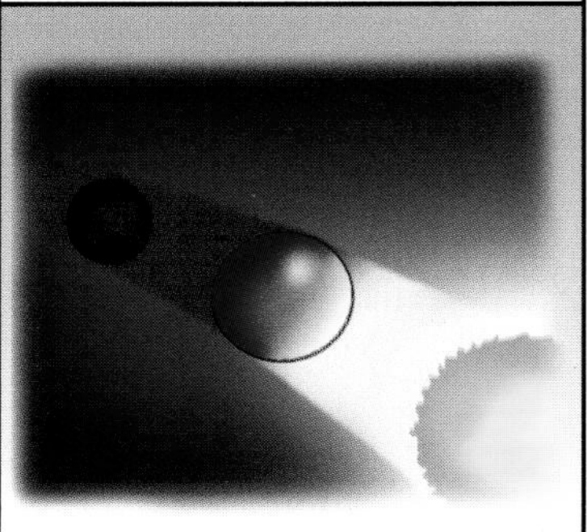

eclipse
ग्रहण
grahaṇ

flood
बाढ़
bā̂dh

fog
धुंध
dhundh

globe
गोल मानचित्र
gōl mān
chitra

lightning
बिजली चमक
bijlī chamak

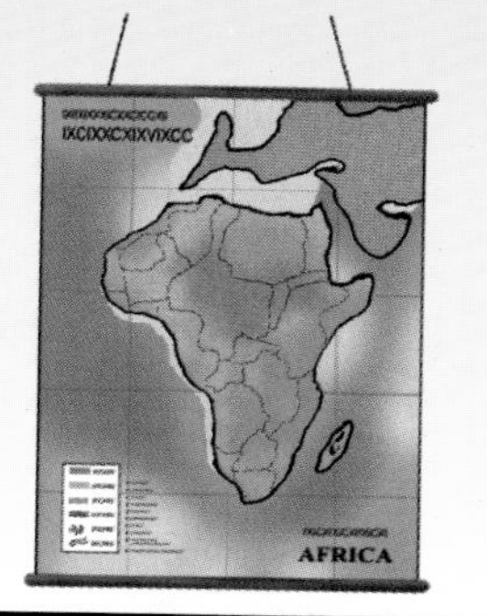

map
नक्शा
nakshā

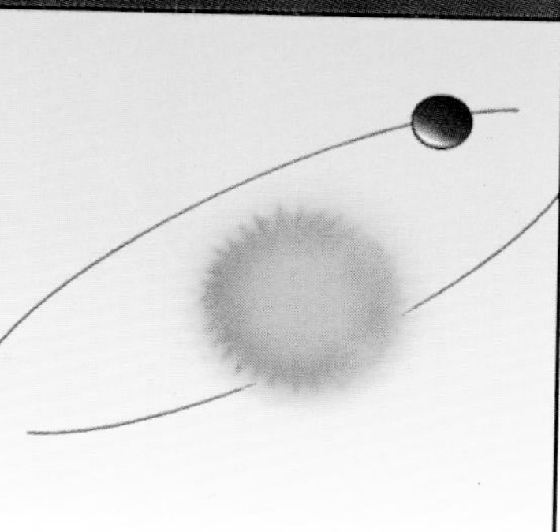

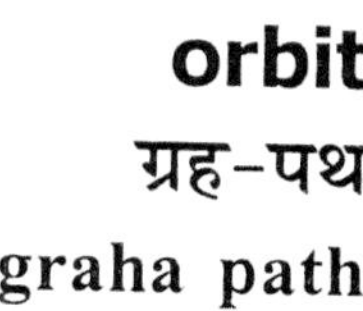

orbit
ग्रह-पथ
graha path

rain
वर्षा
varshā

satellite
उपग्रह
upgrah

sky
आकाश
ākāsh

snow
बर्फ
barph

space
अंतरिक्ष
antariksh

spring
बसंत
basant

storm
तूफ़ान
tūfān

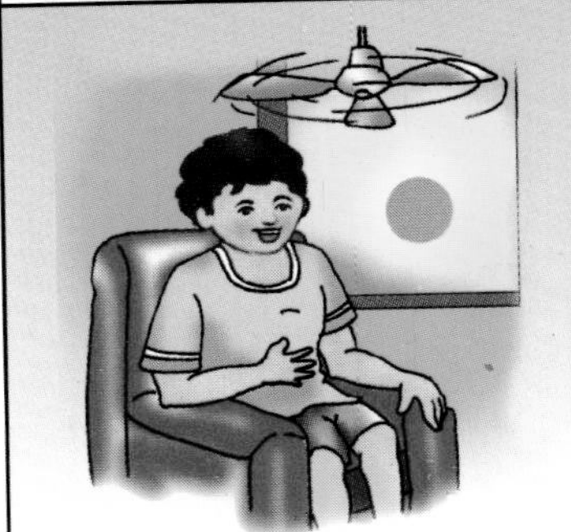

summer
ग्रीष्म ऋतु
grīshma ritu

sun
सूर्य
sūrya

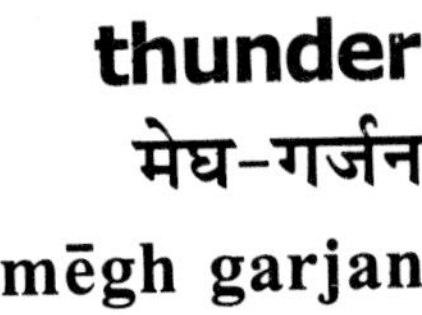

thunder
मेघ-गर्जन
mēgh garjan

tornado
तूफ़ान
tūfān

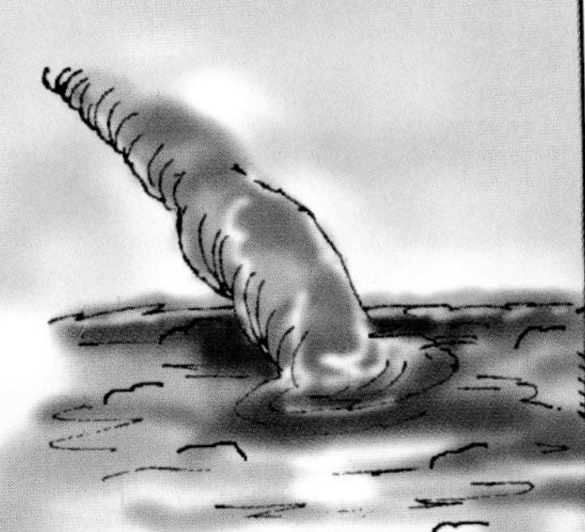

typhoon
बवंडर
bavaṇḍar

volcano
ज्वालामुखी
jvālāmukhī

winter
शीत ऋतु
shīt ritu

OTHER USEFUL WORDS

अन्य उपयोगी शब्द

anya upayōgī śhabd

album
एल्बम
albam

barrel
पीपा
pīpā

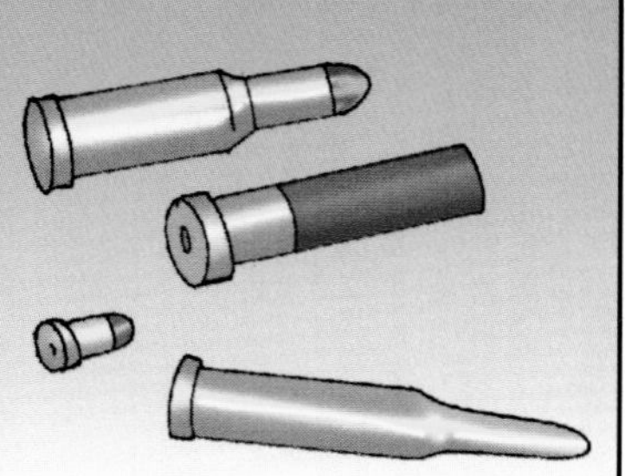

ammunition
गोला बारूद
gōlābārud

basket
टोकरी
ṭōkari

axe
कुल्हाड़ी
kulhāḍī

battery
बैटरी
baiṭarī

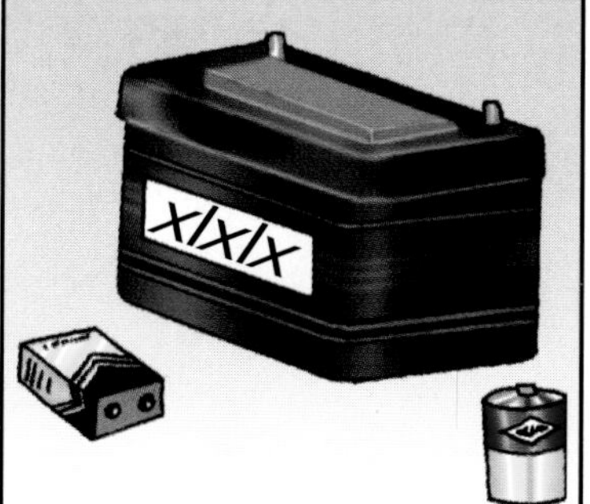

badge
बिल्ला
billa

bell
घंटी
ghaṇṭi

bag
थैला
thailā

book
पुस्तक
pustak

bottle
बोतल
bōtal

box
संदूक
sandūk

bricks
ईंट
īnṭ

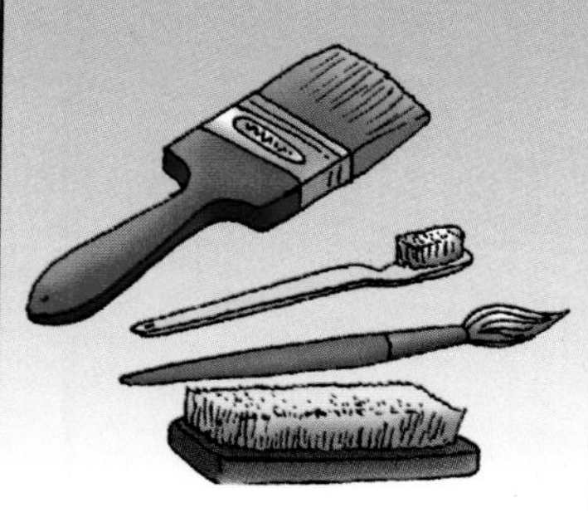

brushes
ब्रुश
brush

belt
पेटी
pēṭī

buttons
बटन
baṭan

cable
बिजली की तार
bijlī ki tār

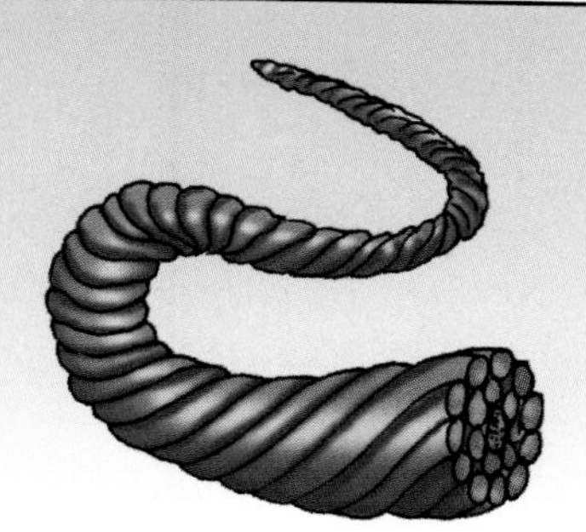

cage
पिंजरा
piñjarā

camera
कैमरा
kaimarā

candle
मोमबत्ती
mōmbattī

playing cards
ताश
tāsh

coins
सिक्के
sikkē

chain
जंजीर
jañjīr

combs
कंघी
kaṅghī

cheque
चैक
chaik

computer
कम्प्यूटर
kampyūṭar

clock
घड़ी
ghaḍ̂ī

cord
डोरी
ḍōrī

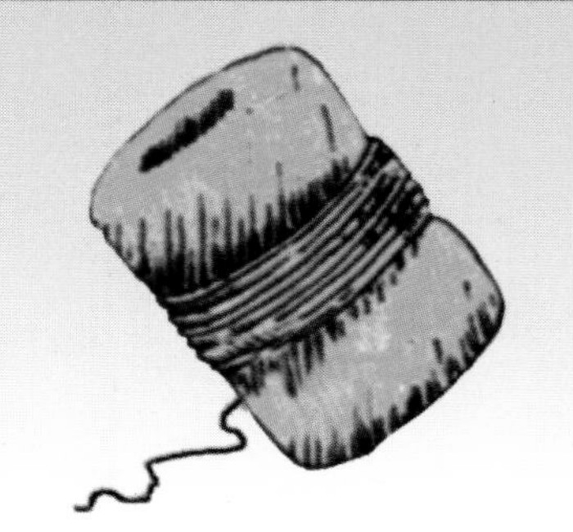

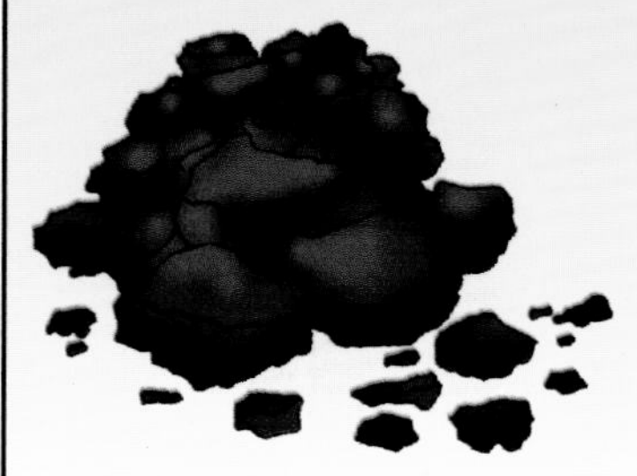

coal
कोयला
kōyalā

cushions
गद्दे
gaddē

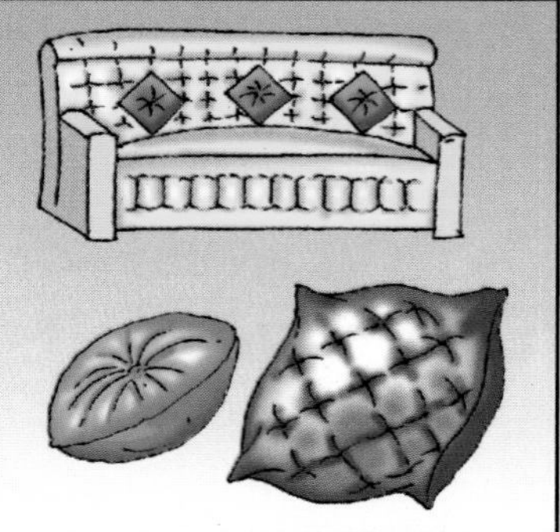

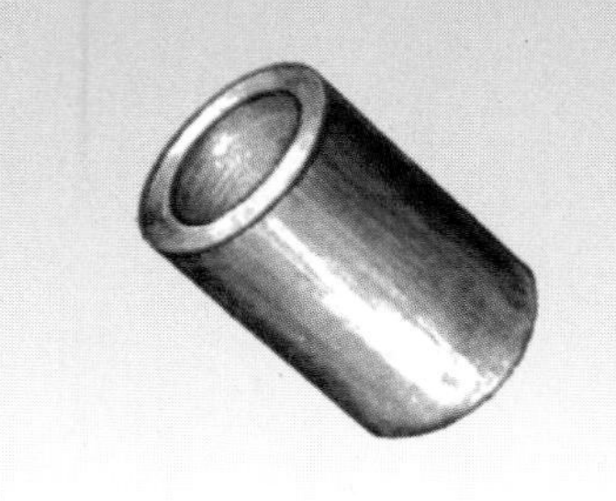

cylinder
सिलिंडर
silinḍar

dagger
कटार/खंजर
kaṭār/
khanjar

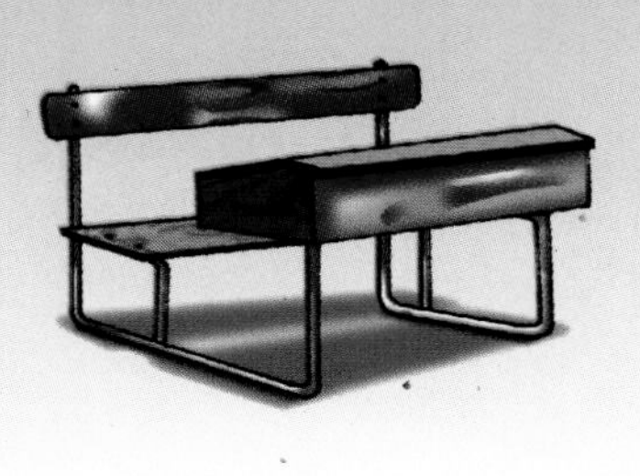

desk
छोटी मेज़
chhōṭī mēz

dish
तश्तरी
tashtarī

drawer
दराज़
darāz

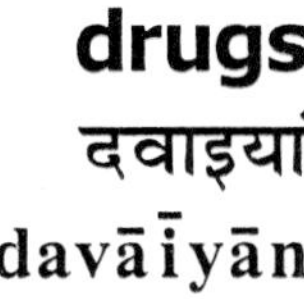

drugs
दवाइयां
davāīyān

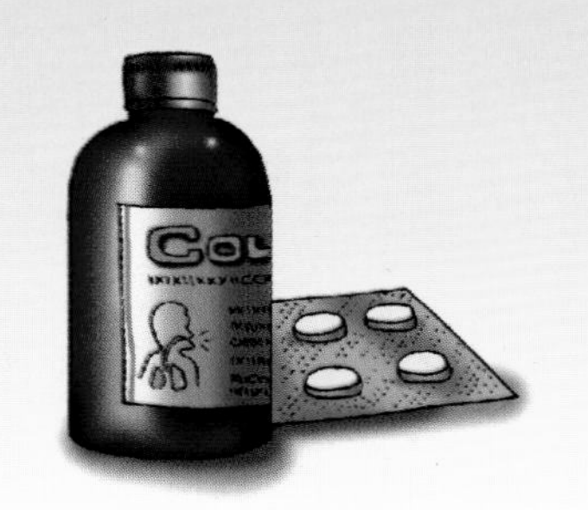

dustbin
कूड़े दान
kūḍēdān

envelope
लिफ़ाफ़ा
liphāphā

eraser
रबड़ (मिटाने
वाला)
rabaḍ

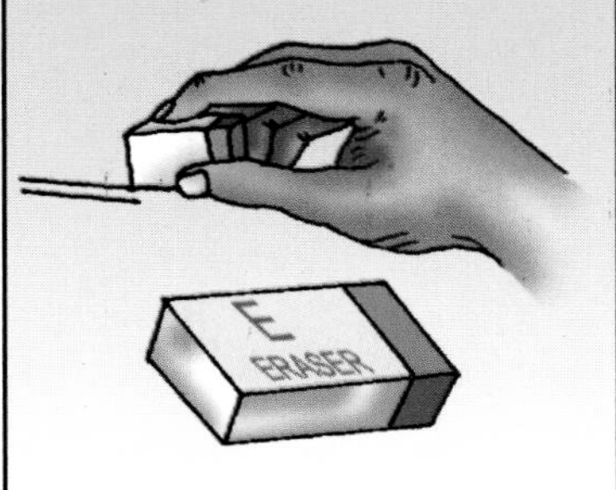

fan
पंखा
paṅkhā

fire
आग
āg

flag
झंडा
jhaṇḍā

fountain
फव्वारा
phavvārā

fur (coat)
फर कोट
phar kōṭ

garbage
कूड़ा
kūḍā

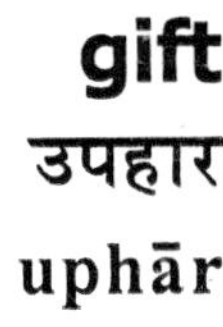

gift
उपहार
uphār

glass
शीशा
shisha

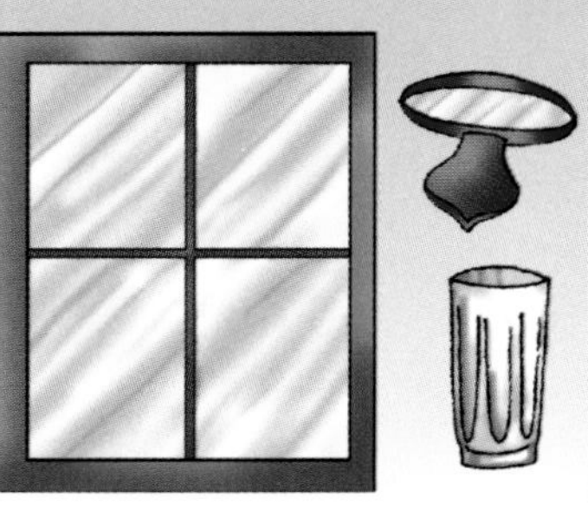

gloves
दस्ताने
dastānē

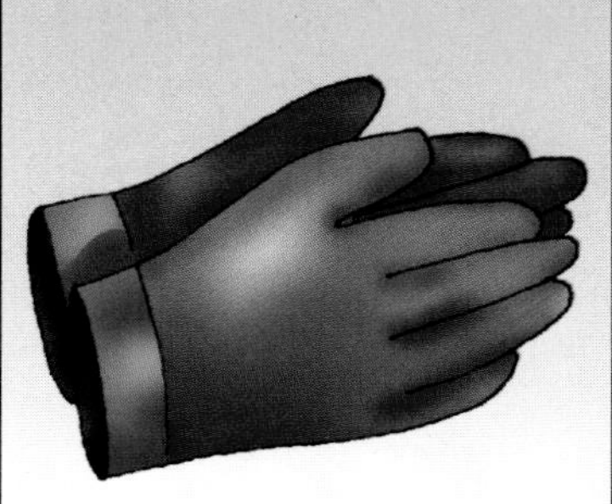

goblet
प्याला
pyālā

goggles
धूप चश्मा
dhūp
chashmā

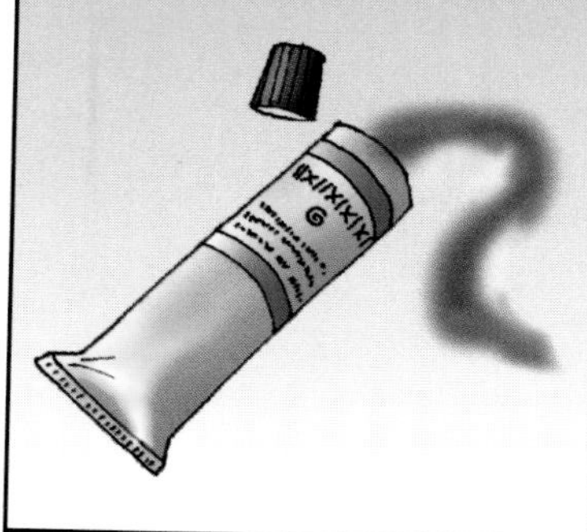

gum/glue
गोंद
gōnd

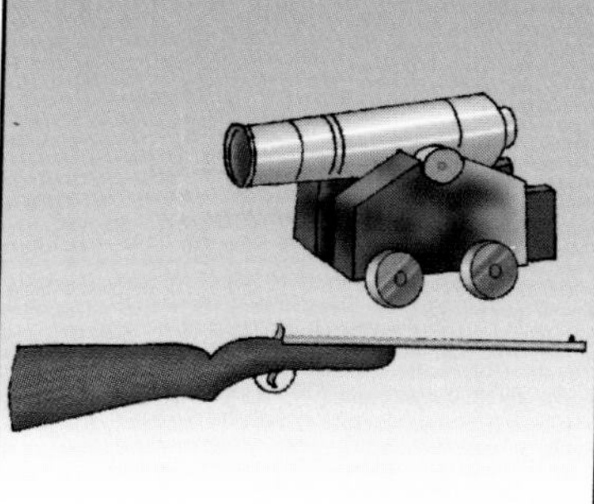

guns
बन्दूक
bandūk

hammer
हथौड़ा
hathauḍa

handker-chief
रूमाल
rūmāl

handle
हत्था
hatthā

hats
टोप
ṭōp

helmet
सुरक्षा टोप
surakshā ṭōp

ink
स्याही
syāhī

ivory
हाथी दाँत
hāthī dānt

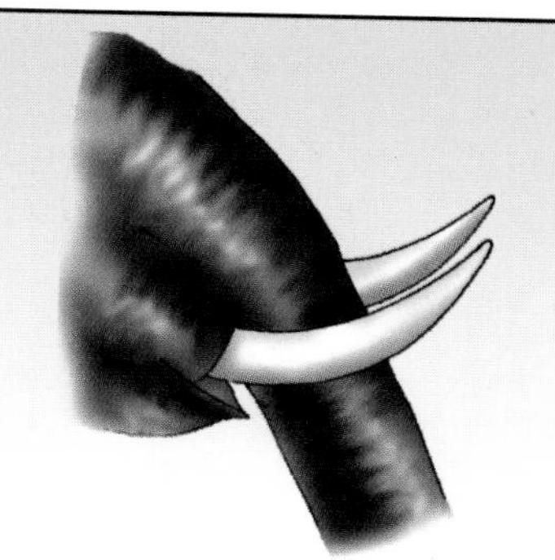

jar
मर्तबान
martbān

jug
जग
jag

kettle
केतली
kētalī

keys
चाबियां
chābiyān

knives
चाकू
chākū

label
लेबल
lēbal

lace
तस्मा, फ़ीता
tasmā, phītā

ladder
सीढ़ी
sīd̂hī

leather
चमड़ा
chamad̂ā

lens
सूक्ष्मदर्शी शीशा
sūkshmadarshī
shisha

letter
पत्र
patr

lock
ताला
tālā

luggage
सामान
sāmān

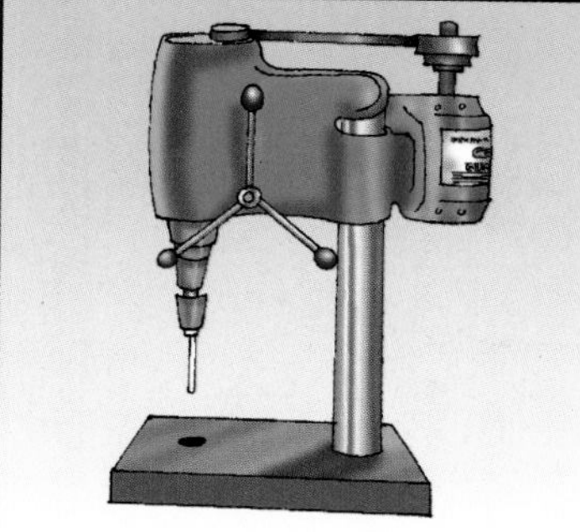

machine
यंत्र
yantra

masks
मुखौटा
mukhauṭā

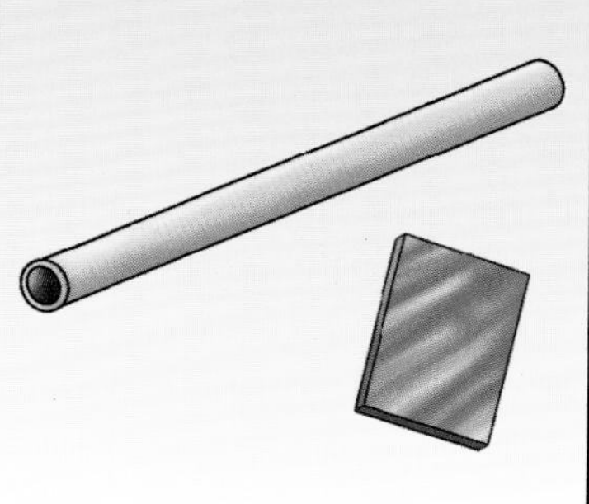

metal
धातु
dhātu

mirror
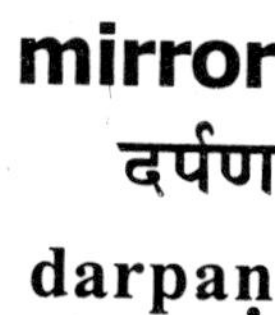
दर्पण
darpaṇ

money
धन
dhan

mud
कीचड़
kīchad̂

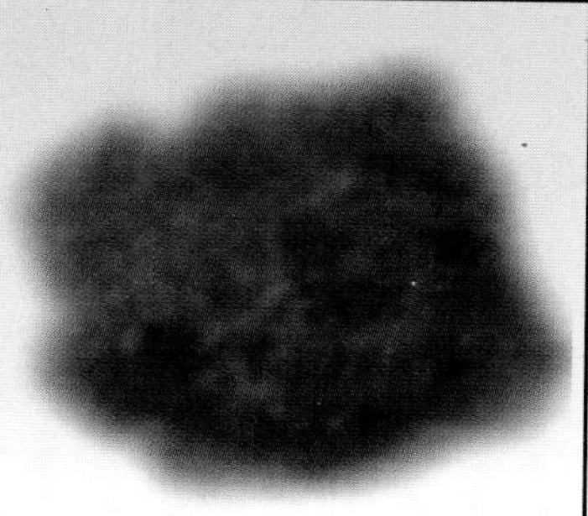

mug
प्याला
pyālā

napkin
छोटा तौलिया
chōṭā tauliyā

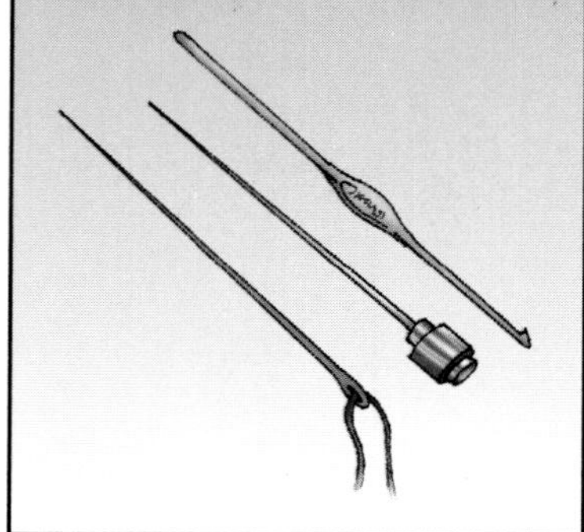

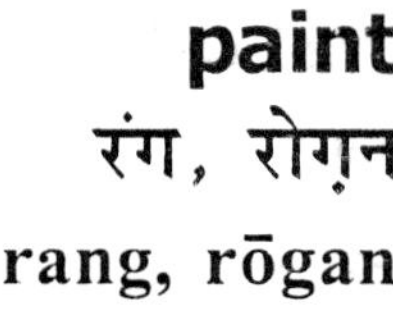

needles
सुई
sūī

nest
घोंसला
ghōnsalā

net
जाल
jāl

newspaper
समाचार पत्र
samāchār
patr

oil
तेल
tēl

paint
रंग, रोग़न
rang, rōgan

parcel
पार्सल
pārsal

pedal
पैडल
paiḍal

pen
कलम
kalam

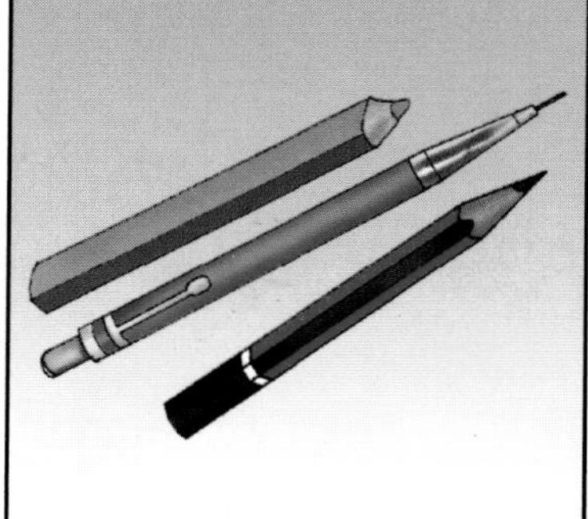

pencils
पेन्सिल
pēnsil

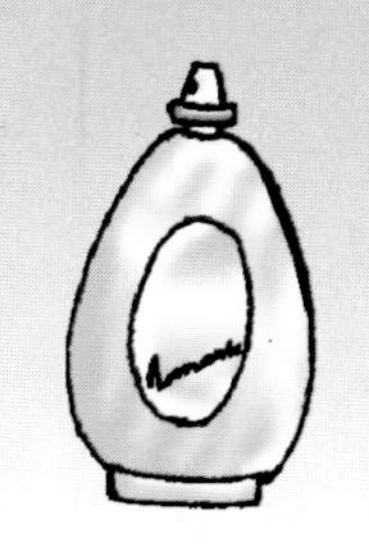

perfume
इत्र
itr

photograph
फोटो
phōṭō

painting
तस्वीर
tasvīr

pillow
तकिया
takiya

pistol
पिस्तौल
pistaul

plate
तश्तरी
tashtarī

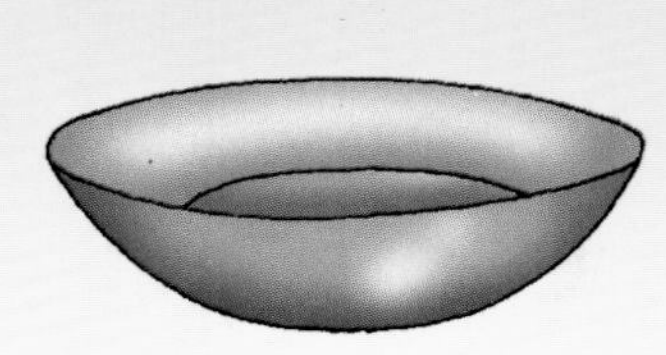

pot
बर्तन
bartan

powder/ talcum
पाउडर
pāuḍar

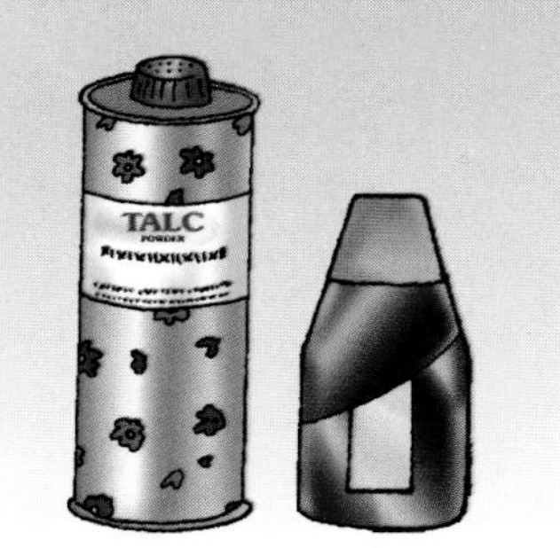

pump
पम्प
pump

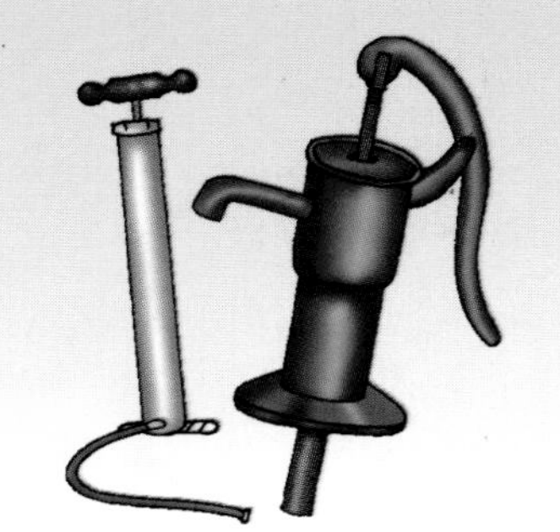

purse
बटुआ
baṭuā

quilt
रज़ाई
razāī

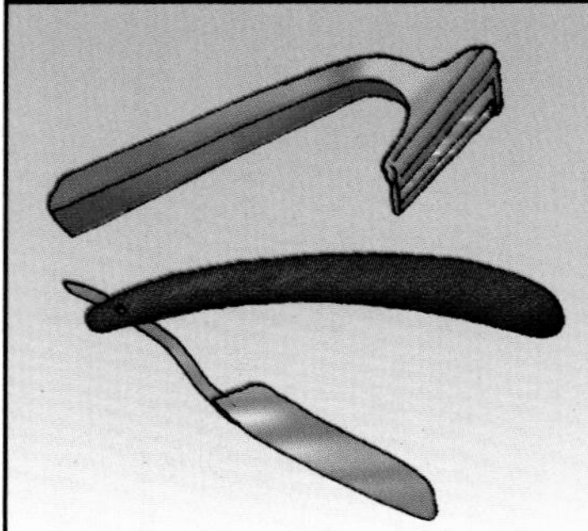

razors
उस्तरे
ustarē

refrigerator
रेफ्रिजरेटर
rēphrijarēṭar

register
रजिस्टर
rajisṭar

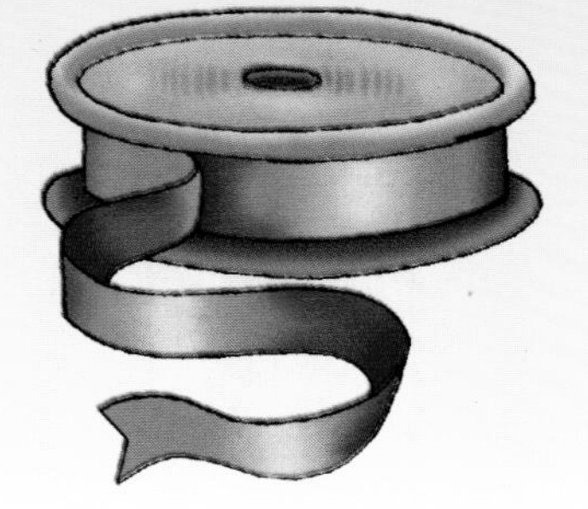

ribbon
फीता
phītā

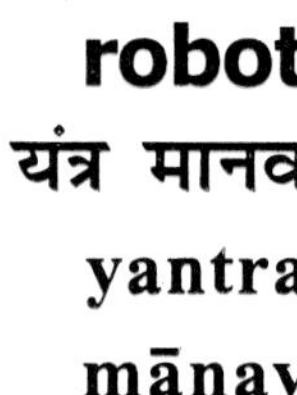

robot
यंत्र मानव
yantra
mānav

roll
रोल
rōl

rope
रस्सी
rassī

sacks
बोरे
bōrē

saw
आरा
ārā

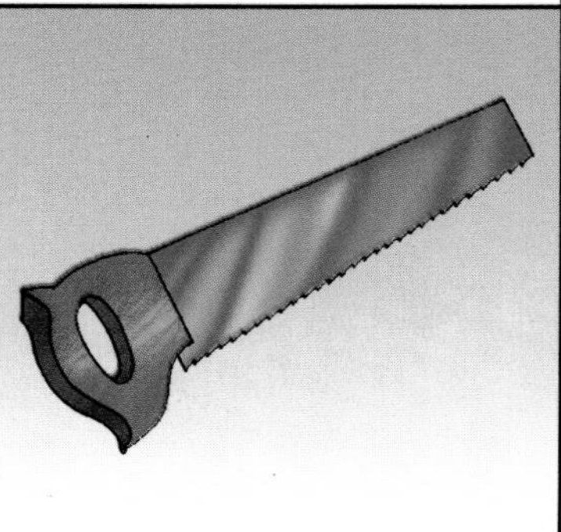

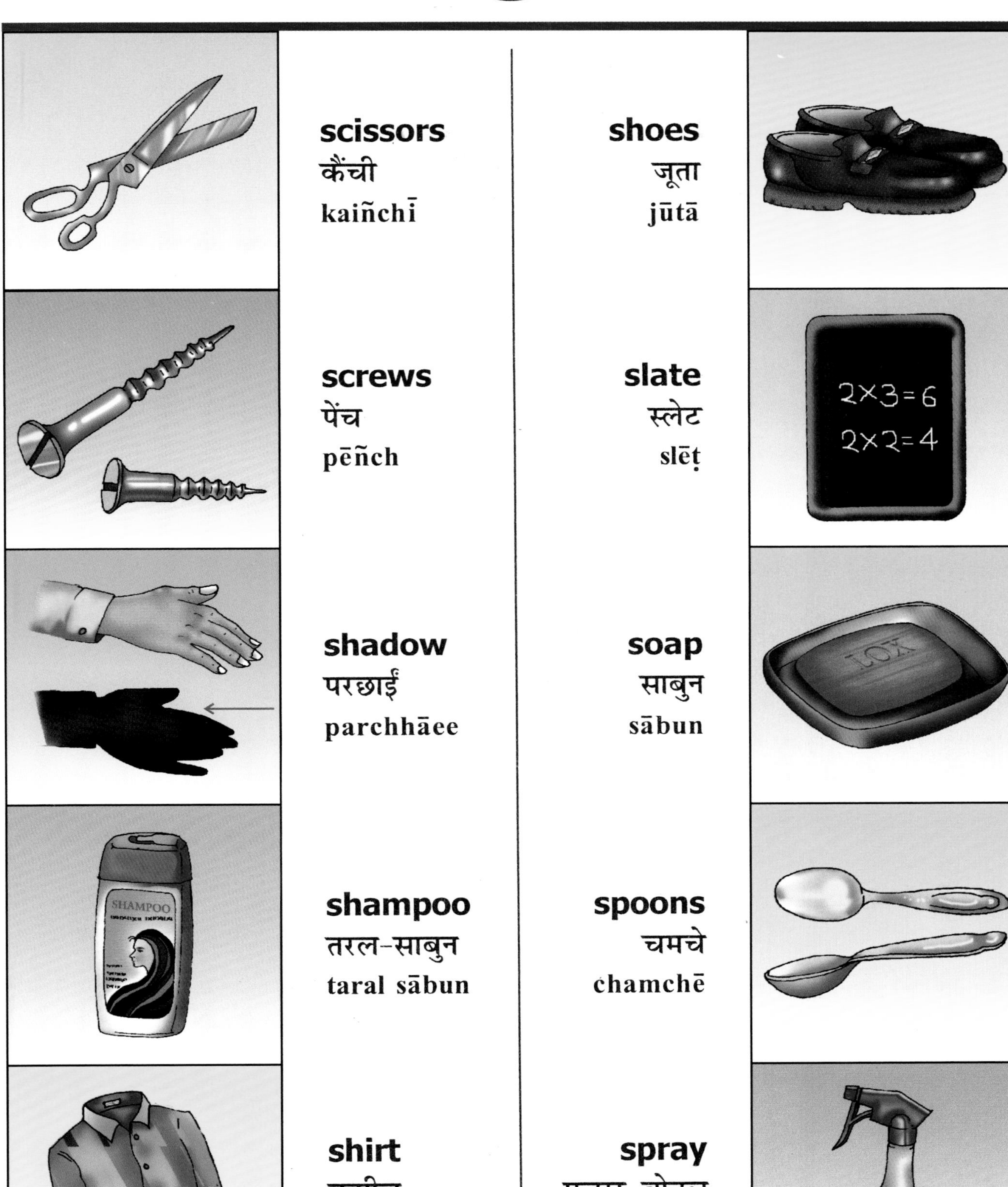

scissors
कैंची
kaiñchī

screws
पेंच
pēñch

shadow
परछाईं
parchhāee

shampoo
तरल-साबुन
taral sābun

shirt
कमीज़
kamīz

shoes
जूता
jūtā

slate
स्लेट
slēṭ

soap
साबुन
sābun

spoons
चमचे
chamchē

spray
फुहार बोतल
phuhār bōtal

statue
मूर्ति
mūrti

ticket
टिकट
ṭikaṭ

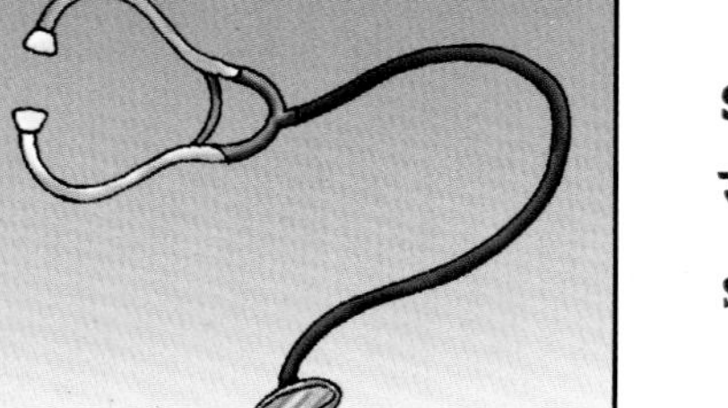

stethoscope
स्टेथिस्कोप
sṭēthiskōp

timber
इमारती लकड़ी
imāratī
lakad̂ī

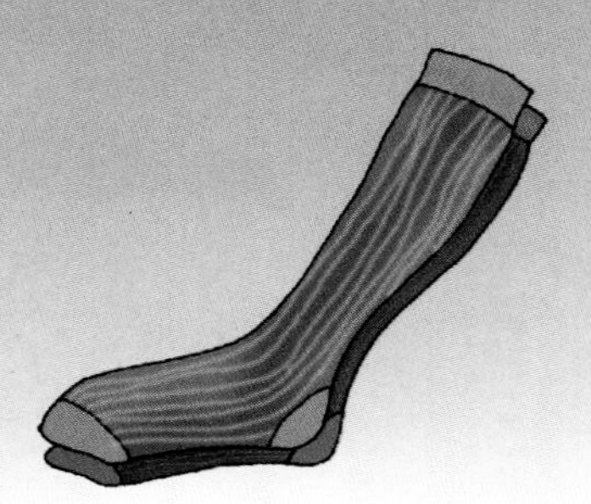

sock
जुर्राब, मोज़ा
mōza, jurab

tins
डिब्बा
ḍibbā

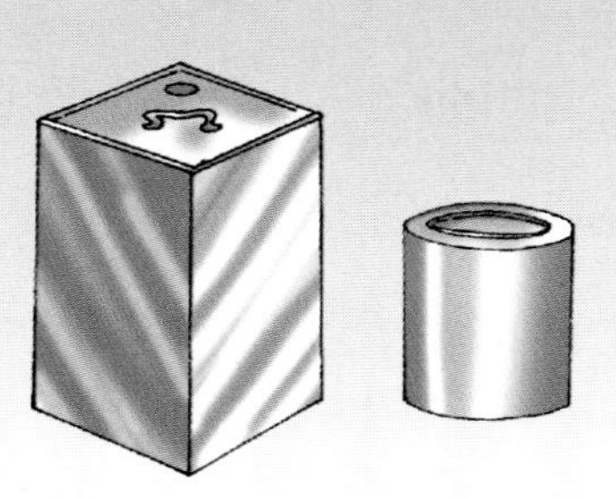

teapot
केतली
kētalī

tools
औज़ार
auzār

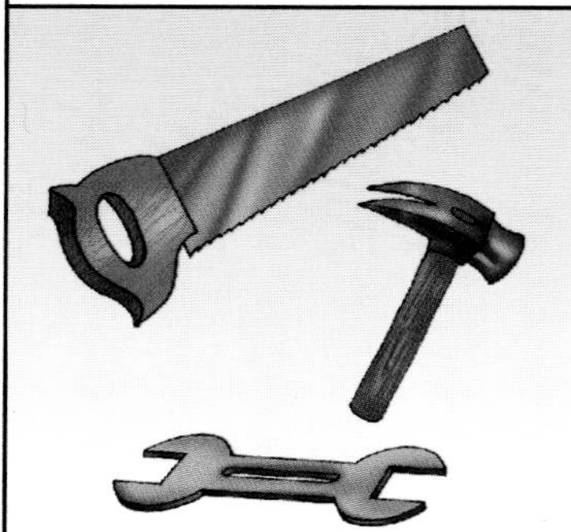

thread
धागा
dhāgā

towel
तौलिया
tauliyā

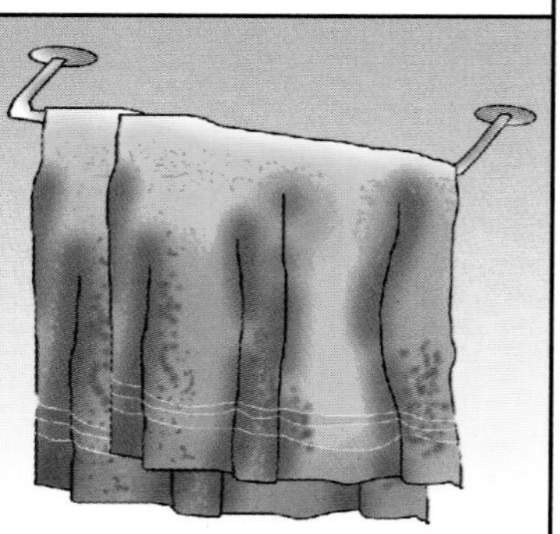

mouse-trap
चूहे का फन्दा
chūhe ka phandā

tray
थाली
thālī

treasure
खजाना
<u>kh</u>ajānā

tubes
ट्यूब
ṭyūb

turban
पगड़ी
pagaḓī

typewriter
टाईप-मशीन
ṭāīp maśhīn

umbrella
छाता
chhātā

utensils
बर्तन
bartan

vaseline
वेज़लीन
vēzalīn

vault
तिजोरी
tijorī

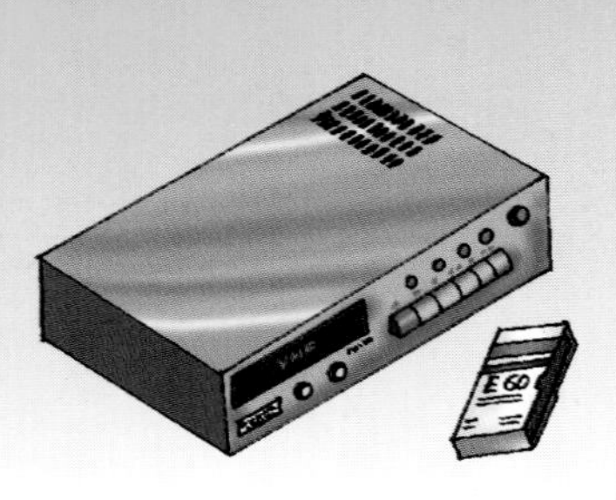

video machine
विडियो मशीन
viḍiyō mashīn

wallet
बटुआ
baṭuā

washing-machine
कपड़ा धुलाई मशीन
kapad̂ā dhulāī mashīn

watch
घड़ी
ghad̂ī

weapons
अस्त्र
astr

web
मकड़ी-जाल
makad̂ī jāl

wings
पंख
paṅkh

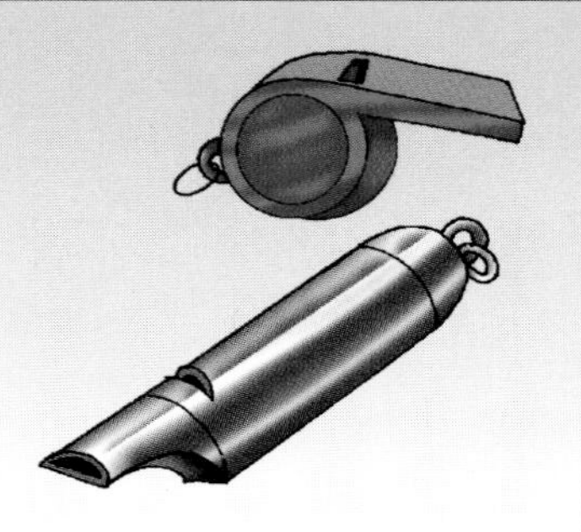

whistles
सीटियां
sīṭiyān

wool
ऊन
oon

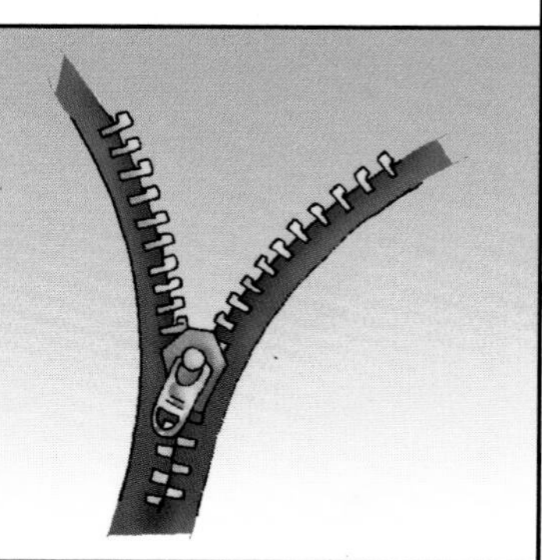

zipper
जिप
zip